...a thousand words

...a thousand words

Spiritography and the Book of Portraits

Jim DeCaro

Copyright © 2024 James DeCaro

All Rights Reserved

No part of this work may be reproduced in any form without written permission from the publisher.

This is a work of nonfiction.

All photographs and images by JD

Cover Design by JD

ISBN 979-8-9901669-0-5

Library of Congress Control Number: 2024905758

First Edition
2024

Spiritography Publishing Company
Connecticut USA

www.spiritography.com

…of course it's dedicated to my wife.

ACKNOWLEDGMENTS

I would like to thank you for reading my book.

"Thank You"

CONTENTS

* Foreword *

* Preface *

* Introduction to Spiritography *

* Apparitions *

* Book of Portraits *

* Diary of a Madman *

* Afterword *

* Appendices *

Table of Contents

Foreword - Raymond A. Moody, M.D. xvii
Preface xxv
Introduction to Spiritography 01
Apparitions 09
    Hun-Tdey 12
    A Tear in Space 15
    The Ole Man 17
    Elle 22
    Experiments with Nighttime Photography 24
    The Other Side of the Lens 35
        Ectoplasm: theory of emanations 35
        DNA Factor 39
Book of Portraits 49
    T-Bone 71
    Wyatt 74
    Fingers 77
    King Dragon 80
    James 83
    Djra-Kul-A-Din 85
    Chief 86
    Endora 88
    Fang 89
    Beast of the Angels 90
    Instant Karma 91
    Lord of the Seven Days 92
    Sparx 94
    Wings of the Wind 95
    John the Elder 97
    Hammerhead 98
    Flag 99
    ChilliPop 100
    The Drip 101
    Aquadio 102
    Spirit of the Second Sight 103
    Dr. Seven 104
    Ace 105
    Karats 106
    Prince Dragon 107
    Bones 108

Diary of a Madman 113
  Now You've Seen What I've Seen 113
  The Creeps 117
  Theater of the Mind 121
  Psychic Eye Radio 123
  A Shared Space 127
  The Devil 'sin the Details 135
Afterword 143
APPENDICES 149
  Appendix A: Table of Photographs/Images 150
  Appendix B: Spiritography 152
  Appendix C: Cameras / Computers / Digital Equipment 153
  Appendix D: Bibliography / References 154
  Appendix E: Sunrise 155
Index.. 165

...a thousand words

Pantheon of American Spiritography

Immortals
Spirit Entities
Wandering Souls
Supernatural Intelligence

"The images evoke a convincing feeling of seeing into an alternate plane of existence..."

Raymond A. Moody, M.D.

Foreword

Foreword

Raymond A. Moody, M.D.

A New Technique for Spirit Communication

When Jim and I got together to view his spirit photographs, I was immediately impressed. I explained to him that I was ignorant about cameras and photography, so could not comment on that dimension of his work. What impressed me were the nature of the images themselves, and the process by which the mind attempted to make sense of them. In fact, what Jim's work taps into is one of the most exciting forms of visionary experience and transcendent consciousness: pareidolia.

On one level, pareidolia is the mental process involved in seeing faces and other shapes and figures in clouds. Yet, on another level, people instinctively relate pareidolia to the transcendent dimension of life, and imbue it with profound spiritual meaning. And Jim's technique of spirit photography, whatever it may involve, opens up virtually endless possibilities of pareidolic visions. It promises to give people easy access to a domain of the spiritual life that is ordinarily excluded from awareness, except under extraordinary circumstances. It even makes it possible to create a book in which readers could view images of their own deceased loved ones!

As I rushed through all these points, I could mentally hear Jim saying "Whoa!" Admittedly, it all sounded wildly implausible, although it is demonstrably true. So, I had to back up and start with some basics of anomalistic psychology—the study of remarkable mental phenomena that challenge everyday concepts of reality.

Seeing faces in clouds, a visionary experience familiar to most children, is an example of the type of visual illusion known as pareidolia. It is classified as an illusion because it is brought about by the mind's interpreting an objectively observable but ambiguous stimulus could be clouds, or smoke, of fog, or flames, or ill-defined shadows, or the like. Or, it could even be a solid object, like the complex shading and grain patterns in a wooden door or wall. Or, as in the present case, the stimulus could be the complex whirls and dappled patterns Jim somehow captured with his camera. The stimulus then engages a strange perceptual process that remains a real mystery of the mind, however familiar it may be. For, to refer to pareidolia as an illusion does not imply that it is necessarily unreal. After all, human beings have always put their remarkable capacity for pareidolic vision to use for spiritual and supernatural purposes.

Certain Native American groups, for example, used pareidolia for divination–seeing into the future. Specifically, they practiced capnomancy, gazing into clouds of smoke billowing from the medicine man's ceremonial fire. By interpreting the images he saw in the puffs and swirls of smoke, the shaman could surmise what the days to come had in store for his people. Even today, certain indigenous tribes in Central America still practice capnomancy.

Pareidolia is also the basis of a baffling type of collective visionary phenomena often reported in news media. When Jesus' face is seen peering out from the wood grain of a hospital door, or the Virgin Mary is observed on the plate glass window of a bank, pareidolia is at work. Once one of two people notices an unusual image of that kind, and brings it to the attention of others, word about the seemingly miraculous manifestation spreads like wildfire. Soon, people are flocking to the spot from all over the world hoping to experience the living presence of the divine.

At such scenes, even those who come mainly to scoff can become noticeably reverent in their demeanor. For the images of pareidolia can appear startlingly real, real enough to make someone pose the big, spiritual questions. Somehow, pareidolia has a stupendous power to engage the transcendent propensities of humankind. And who among us can say with certainty that spirits or divine entities would not choose to communicate with us through a perceptual process that is present in almost everyone? At any rate, those who are transported by pareidolic visions certainly feel they are in contact with some higher plane of reality. Who is to say they are not?

Besides, pareidolia is unlike other common illusions in a corspicious and important way. Consider, for example, the experience of seeing illusory intruders in one's home at night. Almost everyone has been startled by what appeared to be an unknown person lurking ominously in a darkened room. Then, as soon as one pays close attention to it, the figure instantly dissolves into a hat and overcoat hanging harmlessly from a wall hook. In short, most visual illusions simply disintegrate when one looks at them closely.

Pareidolia is not like that though. One of the primary characteristics of pareidolic visions is that the more one looks at them, the more real they seem to become. What is more, the viewer can point such a vision out to others, and then they can see it, too! No wonder pareidolia frequently results in profound, life-changing, visionary experiences.

George Patton was a great American military hero who was descended from a long line of great American military heroes. The young Patton had his transformative pareidolic vision during a fierce battle in World War I, long before he gained fame with his exploits as a combat general. At a crucial moment in the battle, Patton was almost sure to be killed. He rallied his courage when he looked up into the sky and saw the faces of his military hero ancestors looking down upon him from the clouds. Patton experienced what he definitely felt was actual contact with the spirits of departed relatives through the amazing medium of pareidolia. As far as I know, no "skeptics" ever confronted General Patton and dismissed his spiritual experience as the mental wanderings of a fantasy –prone personality.

Jim DeCaro's work brings home to the millions a form of contact with the spirit world that George Patton glimpsed during a battlefield crisis. For, as one gazes at Jim's spirit photographs, layer after layer of astonishing images emerge. The viewer sees faces as well as full figures of spirit entities, complex scenes, and spiritual presences interacting in groups. The viewer also feels an incredible sense of reality and a kind of uncanny nostalgia. The images evoke a convincing feeling of seeing into an alternate plane of existence, a parallel universe that seems odd and ethereal, yet feels strangely like home.

I was happy to explain to Jim that his technique opens the possibility of enabling virtually everyone to glimpse deceased relatives. If a book had enough images, practically anyone would be able to find a believable portrait of a lost love one. Preparing oneself by looking through old family photographs and reminiscing about those who have passed away would definitely enhance the effect. Then, once someone glimpsed Uncle Ted, or Grandma Annie, the amazing, spiritual power of pareidolia would come into play. The more one looked at the image, the more real it would become, and once it was pointed out to others, they would see it, too.

All in all, I figured that Jim DeCaro had stumbled onto an amazing phenomenon. His technique opens the possibility of creating a gallery of snapshots from the other side, a sort of family album of eternity. And think of the comfort that could bring.

Raymond A. Moody, M.D.

*"The lack of intriguing substance or vision ...as I see it,
remains constant and prevalent amongst current observations:
We deserve better ...and I agree."*

Preface

...a thousand words

Preface

My incentive in writing this book is to share the final results of my experiments in spirit photography. In a way, I feel responsible to share these findings. And yes, it sounds self-serving ...and it gets worse. I have felt this way since the beginning of this project. I knew this material was something special. There was never any doubt to me that I would publish these findings in full, the question was ...when? The answer is ...now.

Firsthand experience is often a welcome approach in obtaining or presenting facts. As well, facts often require corroborative evidence in support of any opinions, especially in a case such as this one. Earlier releases of the photographs and images included in this work were often received in a positive light by most third party observers, experts and non-experts alike. Most judgments favor highly unique qualities ...and I agree.

Over the years, there have been instances where I have shared my work with others, who have chosen to publish it with my blessing. Magazine and book covers, a television documentary, an international peer reviewed academic journal. And now, with this final work, I'm sharing the rest, the good stuff, my stuff, and I'm sharing it ...my way.

I wanted to make myself clear, and I'm running out of time. Inspiration: you'll know it when you get it, just hope you don't regret it. You see, it's not so much inspiration as it is the freedom to even write this book. I think it's obvious a firsthand experience is optimal for an authentic representation of the facts. The inspired conflict must come from within. I've not suffered a shortage of conflict, inspired or otherwise in order to complete this book.

One of my hopeful objectives is to place within the public arena an accurate, authentic, and transparent experience accompanied by unique and abundant supporting evidence. The lack of intriguing substance or vision ...as I see it, remains constant and prevalent amongst current observations: We deserve better ...and I agree.

Honestly, I didn't know how to write a book, this is my first attempt, I'm alone on this one. Much of what I present here often contains: blunt messaging, colorful language, aggression, and other inconsistent expressions of poor judgment and/or questionable behavior patterns.

In my defense, three months after starting this project, I was subjected to six months of weekly chemotherapy treatments ...my cancer is currently in remission. As I said, "I'm running out of time." However, that is not an excuse or a reason for my concept of fair expression.

...no offence intended.

I began writing this work in January 2023. I completed the entire manuscript in December 2023. Final edits were applied in 2024. During that time, I also began work producing a video documentary based on this book. If you like the book, you are gonna' love the video. So for now, enjoy the read.

~ JD ~

*"Several years ago… and several years thereafter,
I wandered the darkness, on the path to the light."*

Portraits 1.1

Introduction to Spiritography

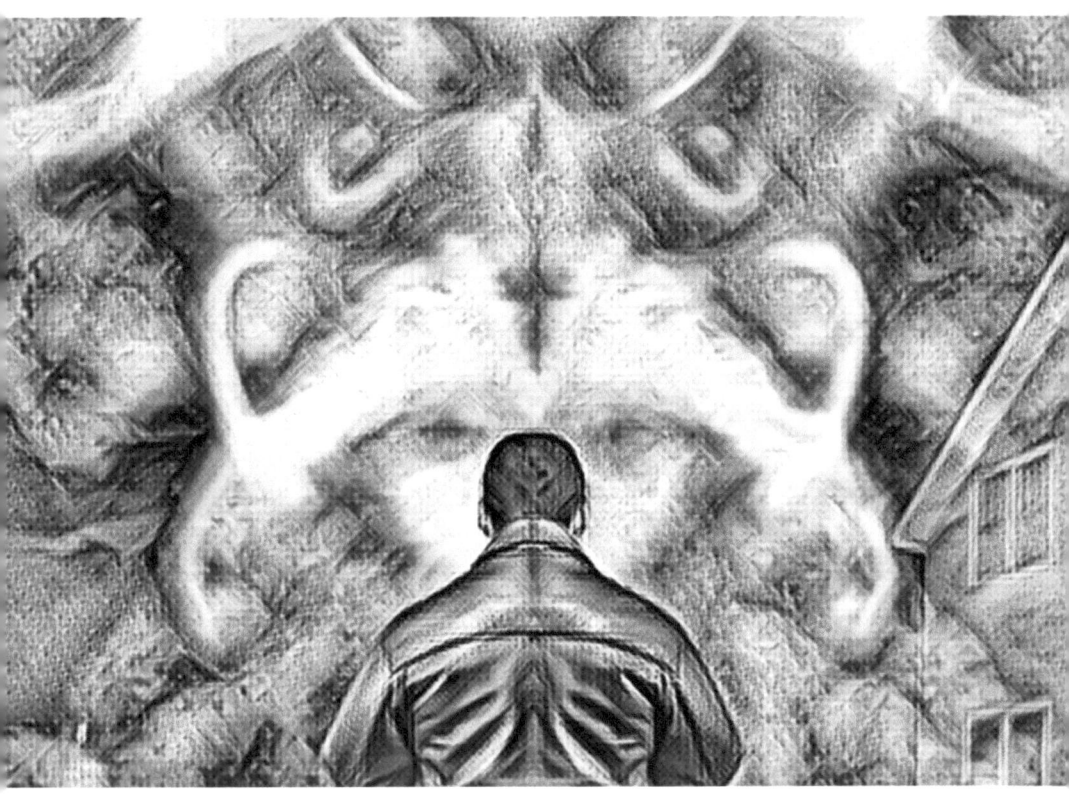

Introduction to Spiritography

What you are about to read is true. It's accompanied by evidential photographs as proof of its truth, accuracy, and authenticity. I'm your host …call me JD. As you will see, what is occurring is a natural or supernatural phenomenon aka an apparition.

I'll get straight to the point. Several years ago, I began to experiment with nighttime photography. The initial objective (photography), covered a 3-5 year period beginning in 1999. During that time, and on numerous occasions, I obtained positive results. To be precise, I could shoot ghosts. It's funny how that sounds, until you actually consider what that means.

I call it "Spiritography." The clearest definition is to say they are illusions derived from photographs of spirit occurrences, but, it's more complicated than that …and simpler too. Is it unexplainable? I'd say it's unbelievable. However, these photographs are the real thing, and because of that, there's a good chance these images may have an effect on your senses. To be honest, I'm expecting that and so should you.

What the reader should keep in mind while reviewing this work, is the countless hours, days, weeks, months and years necessary to acquire this collection of photographs and images. There is no trick, there is no magic, and there is no formula. If there is one word, it would be consistency, in the time I spent alone, in the dark, waiting for something to appear. The problem is, sometimes they do appear, and that's when they get shot. Problem solved.

The Apparitions chapter contains my collection of original, untouched photographs of anomalous phenomena. The Portraits are supernatural illusions. Together they represent the most interesting documented visual phenomenon in spirit research.

At times, I've resigned to offer an explanation when no explanation is available. I don't know if I'm always right, but I try to be. I've seen them, I've heard them and I've captured them. But proceed cautiously, we are dealing with a rare unconfirmed event. It may be supernatural.

They're not always invisible, during the night they appear naturally. I've learned that by waiting alone in the dark, sometimes they would appear. I believe the material in the atmosphere adheres to them like a skin, rendering them momentarily visible. I began experimenting …and I waited.

Perhaps they have an affinity for the land I now own or perhaps they were the demons from my past. Regardless, it was an opportunity to experience firsthand a natural or supernatural phenomenon known to many, but offered to few…it was a chance to shoot a ghost.

For those who have never seen a ghost or spirit, and I'm sure there are many, you have to try to imagine them for what they are, not what you think they are. These entities are not human, and there is no indication they ever were human. That doesn't make them any less real. So then, what are they?

You can put to rest any thoughts of sorcery, witchcraft or magic. Clearly, they are a naturally occurring phenomenon. In fact, it appears they are as individually unique in their race, as we are within our own. If that seems like a loaded statement, I get it, attempting to identify them as a race requires a considerable incentive. I agree. You shall have it.

Sadly, abstract concepts, particularly those involving the supernatural are often misinterpreted to be controversial or the warning signs of instability. I consider that an advantage in this case as the photographic evidence clearly indicates the anomalous appearance of a ghost, spirit, or presence occurring over a sustained period of time.

Witnessing the materialization of a spirit is a unique experience, and isn't experiencing the supernatural what it's all about? There's a feeling that occurs when suddenly dealt a visual stimulus that's antithetical to the concept of what is possible and what is not; it's reactionary. You can't help yourself, you feel it. For me, it hits me in the gut. I still get that feeling …sometimes. These days it's mostly remembrance, at times vividly, other times, not so much.

Photographs are an excellent solution, and difficult to dismiss. They hold up over time. Not only are photographs the visual recording of the actual event, but the image itself may inspire your imagination to unfold. That's a nice way of saying these images may reflect the influence of the original supernatural occurrence that created them.

I've said there are unique properties composing these images. As stated, they may have an effect on your senses. Observers may focus on a property they either see, feel or imagine. Portraits are my interpretation of these photographic properties as I see, feel and imagine them. While observing the Portraits or Apparitions data, steadfast observation may reveal a connection with a favorite personality. I have many favorites.

It's necessary to state these are my opinions. These are not scientific facts. There are no scientific facts. My opinions are based solely upon my own encounters, my photographs, and my firsthand experiences while obtaining them.

...a thousand words

The idea of devoting ones time and energy to an abstract concept such as ghosts and spirits may be considered as pointless, misguided, or self-serving. Regardless, in order to advance the field of spirit research as well as my own self-serving interests, I chose to shoot them, hang them, and now, put them on display.

What this collection of photographs has in common is I'm the one who shot them. I realize that. It's complicated. Spiritography is my collection of original, untouched photographs of anomalous phenomena. As such, I'm confident that many, every, or all of these images portray the appearance of a ghost, spirit or presence. How do I know it's a ghost? I'll get to that.

After twenty five years of consideration, the systematic recovery of a recognizable structure is confidently obvious. And as it turns out, the best explanation is the simplest explanation, they are Spirit formations, you can see it in their faces, I'm just confirming their authenticity.

You have my word(x 1000).

*"Sitting back in my seat, high above the street,
rising up to meet ...the Sun."*

Portraits 2.1

Apparitions

Apparitions

    I subscribe to an old school concept of an apparition. It physically appears and disappears instantly, it may or may not possess recognizable human anatomical characteristics, and there is no scientific or rational explanation for the occurrence.

    I'm not convinced these appearances constitute a definition of post life human beings, or, a discarnate entity. I am, however, objectively convinced this phenomenon can and does occur with varying levels of confidence. To be clear and to avoid confusion, I refer to many of my apparition photographs as ghosts or spirits, but cannot and do not assert or affirm they are by-products of deceased human beings. Simply not knowing exactly what they are, does not negate the fact they are there.

    By recognizing and avoiding unsubstantiated conclusions eventually you realize, there must be another explanation. I like multiverse theory; parallel universes and alternate dimensions. The concept seems to have much to offer when dealing with hypothetical supernatural intelligences.

But, it also occurs to me, this statement may cause some to close this book, and step away. Please don't. Multiverse theory is an interesting but unproven concept. The photographs and the images contained in them are real, and again you realize, there must be another explanation.

I imagine based on what I see in these photographs, there is a shared space among us. It's not in some parallel universe or alternate dimension, its here, in this universe, in this dimension, we can see it. You want answers. I want answers too. There must be another explanation.

Honestly, I don't understand the math that supports alternate dimensions, but I know others do. I imagine somewhere in those formulas are variables supporting inhabitants. Accordingly, the rules governing those inhabitants should also be available through calculation or observation. In cases such as this, the only recourse for information is through observation.

A shared space theory is an interesting concept, particularly when addressing the invisibility problem. Obviously if we can see the anomaly, it's contained in an observable dimension …ours. Alternate dimensions or sub-dimensions are good answers but remain unproven and again require a further explanation. The questions still remain; who are they? And, where are they from?

One possibility is "the line", the guarded line, it's the place we can't cross over for fear of ever returning, no one ever has.

Imagine for a moment that line exists, physically. It's not difficult to imagine there is a natural barrier separating two consciously intelligent species, something keeping everyone in their respective lane. For instance, there's the water world.

And then, there's the spirit world; an area seemingly inhabited by ethereal entities composed of dynamic atmospheric properties. Of course, the physical properties and intelligence options would differ from those of the water world, and our world as well. One interesting aspect of this concept is these atmospheric anomalies do not appear to possess or require organics to support their conscious intelligence.

Another possibility is the sighted anomaly wandered into the proximity of an initiate at a time when the ectoplasm phenomenon was taking effect. What does that infer? I'll explain. Of course I've read past writings about ectoplasm and the deceptive practices surrounding efforts to produce it. This case is different, no one is trying to trick you, and there is no deception. The issue here is to explain an inexplicably rare phenomenon that remains unexplainable.

Ectoplasm: theory of emanations is interesting but remains an unproven option. I will however attempt to explain the ectoplasm phenomenon as I see it, as I remember it, and as I imagine it. I'll say it again, I don't know if I'm always right, but I try to be.

The phenomenon occurs between sundown and sunrise. They come from within the darkness, and before you jump to any conclusions let me explain…

I think there may be a trigger; a stimulus affecting the psychological element of the initiate such as a camera flash, which in turn triggers a momentary physical response from those anomalies in the surrounding environment. In other words, "caught ya."

From a technical perspective, they were simply outdone by the speed of a camera flash. This option offers much to the imagination, and for many that's good enough. It does not however, explain the positioning of the camera, the quantity of captured anomalies, or the complexity of materialization. Those occurrences may be coincidental and require further evidence to support a determination of supernatural origin …you shall have it.

I base my opinions on my observations, my recorded data, and an abstract sense of logic and reason. I have included within, a substantial, uncorrupted and righteous collection of original photographs that will not only dismay many, but it will haunt you as well.

These are the ones who watch us, who rule us, who haunt us… I captured many of them. I shot them. And then, if they were worth the effort, I hung them. That is a fact …and a true story.

Hun-Tdey

Late one night, in October 1999, I shot Hun-Tdey. As I fired off the flash, he lit up like a candle. I saw his face first, he was staring right at me. We stood face to face and eyeball to eyeball, at around arms length. Simply put, he got the drop on me …and I knew it. Many thoughts raced through my mind in that moment, including self defense. I may have momentarily crossed the line, but it was a desperate attempt to survive the sudden appearance of death.

It all happened so fast it was a reaction. His appearance was literally instantaneous. Although I've never understood how he got so close to me, I remember quite well my first thoughts, "oh shit, they're fkn real, what have I done?" I thought I was about to die.

I was stunned. I knew he got me. I had no doubt this was a real spirit …and you only see them when you die. I felt my stomach drop.

At first he appeared still, then he started floating towards me, I recognized him immediately. The headdress covered the upper half of his face, and went up and around the top of his skull.

As he floated towards me, I suddenly stopped being scared and got mean. Seriously mean. I was resolved to go down fighting and hit him in his big shiny head with a right. And then, he began floating backwards, and he vanished …and he was gone.

I was lucky to get the shot on camera, but it was truly an incredible phenomenon to witness. After all these years I still think it was an honor to meet the Spirit of Hun-Tdey …no hard feelings about the right, bro, like I said, it was a reaction.

I've often considered several possibilities to explain the occurrence …and yes luck was a factor. In reality, you don't know what to think. On the other hand, I knew I made the shot. I hung him on my wall with the others and kept him there for years …who's crazy now?

It wasn't until I examined the photo that I saw the canine directly under Hun-Tdey's chin. During the event, Hun-Tdey and I were in a stare down, I never noticed the canine. All I can say is "wow." How cool is that. I don't know their story, how could I? All I'm aware of is what I see in the photograph and all I can say is "wow." How cool is that. Is it a wolf? I really don't know.

Two days after shooting this photograph, I had a dream of being visited by this same spirit. This time he was not wearing his mask and headdress. He stood very tall and had a friendly look on his face. I knew it was him, and I wondered why. And then I heard one word several times, "Hun-Tdey." He wanted me to repeat the word, which I did several times until he nodded. I realized he was telling me his name. He smiled and vanished.

I consider the Spirit of Hun-Tdey to be my favorite photograph among the apparitions. I can't say if this is a reflected image of my own spirit, one of my ancestral spirits, or a wandering ghost or spirit.

My first thought was of a wandering entity on the attack. No doubt it would be the initial thought of many others as well. Self preservation is a natural instinct, and so is going down swinging, no harm - no foul.

A later thought was ectoplasm: theory of emanations. From the beginning, I thought this entity came out of me, it's reasonable to assume this is how he got so close, so fast, and face to face. It was like a projection. I realize how fkn strange that sounds, that's because it is strange. It also infers ancestral connections through DNA may be possible. I find that very interesting.

Hun-Tdey appeared in the form of a man, a Native American man, solid in form and radiant white. He appeared directly in front of me at a distance of about three feet. We were literally face to face and aware of each other's presence. He was staring at me, right in the eyes. His appearance only lasted a split second but, the experience will remain forever. The photograph of the event will also remain forever. It is and shall remain evidence of direct and intentional contact between this world and an intelligent being from the spirit world. Period.

A tear in space

It's been dark outside for several hours now, but it hasn't been quiet. I remember this evening well, it was darker than most and I had been waiting about ten minutes when I noticed something about to touch my face. I flinched and saw it floating in midair. I could see through it, like bent glass. It got my attention for a reason so I stood there and faced it, silently, motionless, only my eyes were barely moving …so I could watch it. As it came towards me, my finger was already on the trigger.

Once my eyes adjusted to seeing the anomaly in the darkness, I could easily determine its location and dimensions. From prior experiences I knew to remain as still as possible, the slightest movement usually causes them to disappear.

It hovered about a foot off the ground and expanded and contracted in all directions, almost like it was breathing. I could approximate the size because I could see the edges floating like waves in the air. It was translucent, approximately six or seven feet high and about eight feet wide. It would float forward and backward and side to side while also expanding in and out, gracefully as if to music.

I stood there in amazement thinking, "this is fkn real." I started to grow concerned that I might lose the shot if I didn't fire soon. I waited for the camera to be center mass, I watched it for approximately eight or ten seconds, and then I shot it.

The entire mass seemed to explode when the flash ripped into it. As it exploded it seemed to blow out in all directions, it wasn't the first time I had gotten drenched in spirit matter during a session. It was a good four or five seconds before it completely disappeared. I was lucky enough to get off three good shots.

The first one appears as a partially formed human face in flesh tone. It's a face surrounded by a mostly unformed mass of spirit matter. The flesh tone caught my attention; it looks like he's hiding in there, as if he is peering out through a tear in the fabric of space.

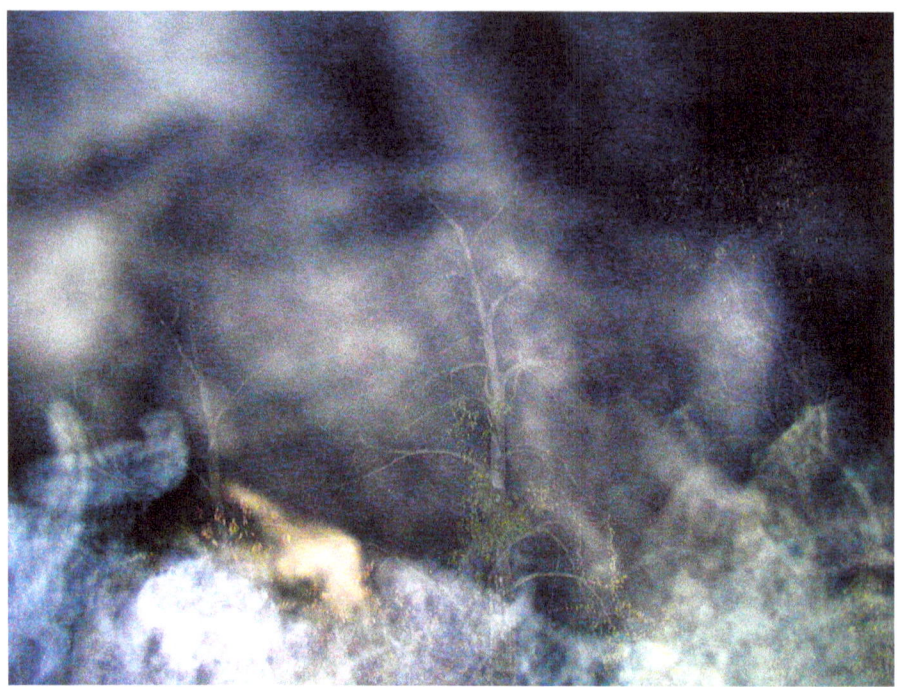

    I never figured out why some apparitions appear more fully formed than others. I'm not convinced it's a matter of timing, especially since I believe I have nothing to do with the timing.

    I've consistently stated, I believe the apparitions appear voluntarily, I'm simply in attendance when the events occur. Therefore, in my mind these occurrences are driven by an unknown force or will that has an agenda or purpose. Apparently, various levels of materialization may be part of that agenda.

    I may be over-thinking that part of the process, it could simply be a random capture. There are however, occasions when intent is a distinct possibility to me, and it can't be ignored. However, if partial formations are intentional, I would imagine it's to make one think, as opposed to settling on the obvious observance. I can get behind that, reason it out, if it's true, to what end or purpose? Does this logic help to propel the concept? For me it does, sometimes, because I consider the possibility of subliminal influencing or messaging.

For instance, the circumstance of this night's occurrence began with something reaching to touch my face. It's possible that the partial face in the photo is the entity that reached out to me and knew how I'd respond, it was just getting my attention.

It's an interesting concept, the amount of time this anomaly remained visible was a rare occurrence, further still, the event resulted in three very strange photographs, also a rare occurrence.

The next shot taken that night is a bizarre scene. I see what appears to be a wizard - a bald headed old man with a white beard and a white robe appears on the right side. On the left, appears to be an adversary, a horned entity, and the two of them are squaring off …that's what I see.

Traditionally, horned deities have been portrayed as being associated with an evil character. With this image, one seems to get the impression of that characterization being an understandable reaction. I imagine one could argue that case with enthusiasm, however, in actuality, it's just a photographic anomaly …a good one.

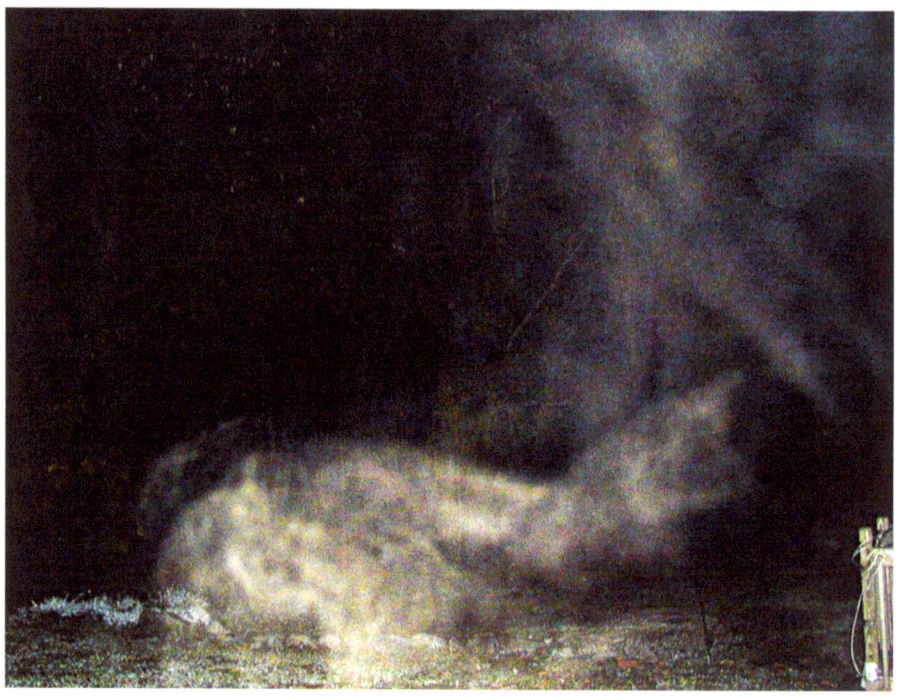

The third anomaly from that session is also a badass image. This photograph was shot just seconds after the prior adversarial photograph. I should add when I'm shooting subsequent to a visual hit, I'm moving my body and the camera in a sweeping motion because they move too. You really get one shot at it, after that its luck when you choose the right direction and get a subsequent hit. In this case I swept to the left and caught it before it vanished. It appears crouched and ready to attack; its head is poised and its jaws are open, I see teeth.

That's all pretty obvious. What you don't see is what he's looking at off camera to the right. Notice the wooden post in the bottom right corner. If you align the second and third photographs using the wood railings-post seen in both photographs, you'll notice the crouched figure in image three is exactly adjacent to the scenario playing out in image two (the wizard). It looks like he's getting ready to jump into the fight …that's good shootin'.

One might notice that I'm not including an image of that scenario of photographs in this sequence. The answer is simple.

The Apparitions section of this book contains only untouched original photographs of the anomalies as they were captured. Other than basic lighting, or contrast settings, these images remain untouched original photographs. However, it really is a cool image, so I've placed a version of the combined images in the appropriate index.

As I mentioned, three apparitions in one night is unusual. But then, so were other circumstances of this particular occurrence. And if you think about it, when is any occurrence not unusual?

At times, I've noticed when you see the anomaly …it moves away, slowly and determinedly. I would get the impression it was watching me as it was retreating, staring at me as if it just read my mind and knew that I saw it. The stare I imagined, was to keep me in my place, it's a momentary occurrence but it usually works. One usually hesitates momentarily when noticing someone staring at them, it's instinct, you stop to look back, and in that moment of hesitation, they're gone. It sounds creepy, but you get used to it, *"like you have a choice."*

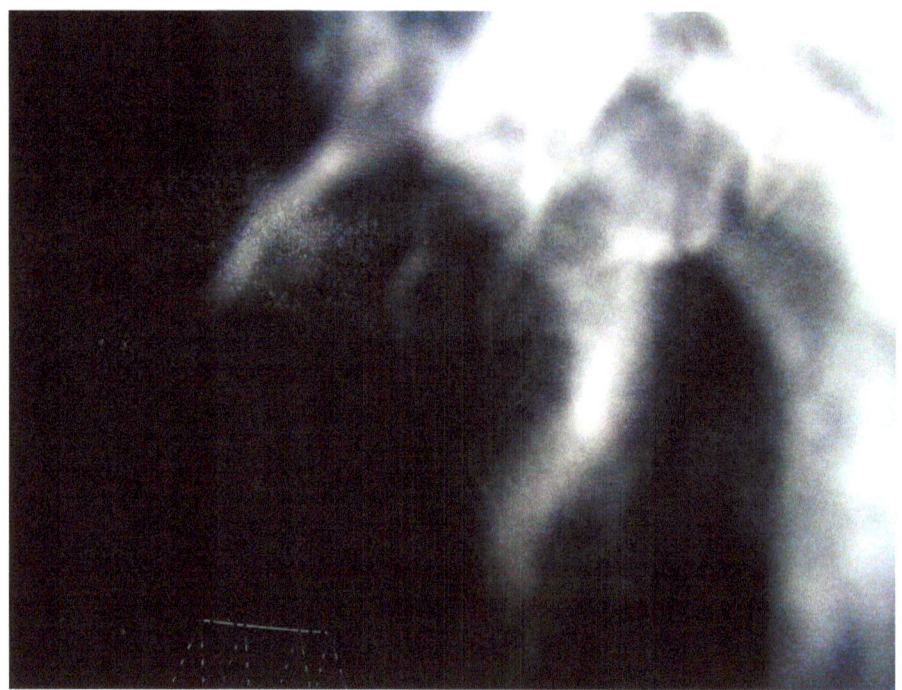

THE OLE MAN

There was a photo session that resulted in an excellent apparition of a man's face looking straight at me, or the camera. Not so funny story behind this photo. It was around this time I got caught up in the Ghosthunter phase that was taking hold in our culture. Reality television and the Internet were quickly adapting to exploit this potentially spiritual phenomenon as a new form of entertainment; Ghost Hunting. Yes, I hunted ghosts. I began by developing my hunting skills, I learned to set traps, and I waited.

One night I was working on a plan for a new trap I conjured up. I felt guilty, I think it was because I knew it would work.

The plan was to get the attention of the local inhabitants. I wanted them to think I was hiding something from them. So I teasingly walked around my yard making it obvious I was trying to hide something in my midsection. It was an adolescent performance at best, however, when I got to the point of - now - shoot. Click.

Well, when I saw that face staring at me I knew it worked, it just wasn't what I was expecting to see. He looked pissed, I wondered if he was aware of my intentions. As I said, I think they can read your mind. I came away with the impression that setting traps is not an agreeable practice between friends.

My original intent was to leave the items as gifts of friendship and respect. For the ladies I left a flower, for the guys I left some booze, some tobacco and a baseball, and for the others I would hide things for them, like cookies or candy, toy soldiers, and baseball cards. Looking back, it may have been a bad choice, or a good one, it depends who you ask. If you ask me, it was worth the time and effort to catch them. Some of it was luck, but some of them were just asking for it. I imagine the spirit I captured that night may have been watching me. What concerned me were the others who were also watching but didn't take the bait.

Two can play that game, so I decided to ignore them.

It's necessary to note, in my opinion, setting a trap to catch a ghost is what a Ghosthunter should do… isn't it? But I don't know, the Ole Man, he sure looks pissed to me.

Elle

There is a ghost that I captured near the old swing set in my yard, I call her Elle. I don't know her real name or where she's from, but to me, the smile on her face is unmistakable, and the red of her lips is almost real. I still wonder what Elle was thinking that made her smile as I shot her. *"sorry, I just couldn't resist that one."*

At first I didn't notice there was another spirit there along with her, if you look down to Elle's left, there is another figure there. She's not as fully formed as Elle, but I see little spirit girl, she's looking right up at Elle's face as if asking to go play on the swings.

I see the souls of two girls playing by a swing set, in the interest of spirit research; the interaction of two souls or spirits is a question many might ask, it's an important factor in understanding the spirit world.

Another question that comes to mind is technical. Why is Elle's apparition somewhat more materialized than her companion? I must claim an unfair advantage in this case, having seen these appearances firsthand. To me, they usually seem to be in motion, both internally and externally, which might explain the different levels of materialization. A directional sweep is how I'd describe it...

As I've seen from these two photographs they resemble us... a little, and us them. Hun-Tdey and Elle appear incredibly lifelike in certain anatomical details, that's because there is no trick and there is no magic, they are photographic anomalies of the natural or supernatural world.

I call them ghosts or spirits because of the facial resemblance to human faces. Whether or not you believe in ghosts, this one is a little tricky, what do you call them?

I call them Hun-Tdey, Elle, and the Ole Man.

Experiments with Nighttime Photography

"Experiments", what do you think that means? To start, it means solitude, plain and simple. "Alone, in the dark, with just your thoughts and a camera." What could go wrong?

Science, logic and reason tell us that ghosts and spirit entities do not exist, so how does a person react if and when they see one? I think fear, shock and the old – bit off more than you could chew syndrome would be accurate. What's the mind's natural reaction in witness to an illogical, unnatural or supernatural event?

In the moments they are visible to the naked eye, most see only vapors if anything at all. And though some appear to explode into the atmosphere, others appear in dead silence. They appear instantly, silently, and then they retreat the same way, it's scary to see it happen.

I wonder if that's the reason we can't agree on their existence, because they scare us too much. They've scared me, but I go after them anyway, because I know they're out there …it's complicated.

...a thousand words

It's mind altering when they physically appear. Seeing one for the first time or any time, I find there's the slightly humbling experience of fear to go along with it. If you were planning on being respectful, now would be the time.

As a cautionary measure I should also add that my photographic experiments always took place outdoors. Assuming the experiments to be successful, and I had no reason to think they wouldn't be, you still run the risk of encountering evil. If shit goes haywire, do you really want that to happen in your house?

It's interesting to note if you attempt to remove the spiritual element from the context of the situation, there is still a physical anomaly which requires an explanation.

What explanation is there for the photograph of Hun-Tdey? Or Elle, or the others? Under what authority is that explanation provided. I'm not convinced anyone can answer that, therefore, you're free to draw your own conclusions, and isn't that what you want? I can provide the facts – you can find your own truth.

There are no external exercises that I employ when attempting to engage the anomalies. I admit I think about it …sometimes, but not always. At times it's like odd thoughts coming out of nowhere, often it's like "hey, check this out" kind of a thing, and then it's gone.

An accurate description of the circumstances involved in the night-time photography sessions is no secret. I have provided that information as faithfully as possible. What I cannot provide is a directive to reproduce the results. Sorry, but you're on your own.

We can discuss habits, processes, rituals, or superstitions. I'm not convinced any of it works, other than the satisfaction one might garner in their own mind. If I were to render an opinion, an inspired thought along with a recognizable emotional response would peak my interest.

In other words: "you wait to be called." If that sounds a little creepy, that's because it is. As a matter of fact the creepier the better, you have to feel it. That's what might draw me outside to begin a photography session. I may or may not have planned the session, but sometimes the draw is strong. That's when I realize this is my recognizable response;

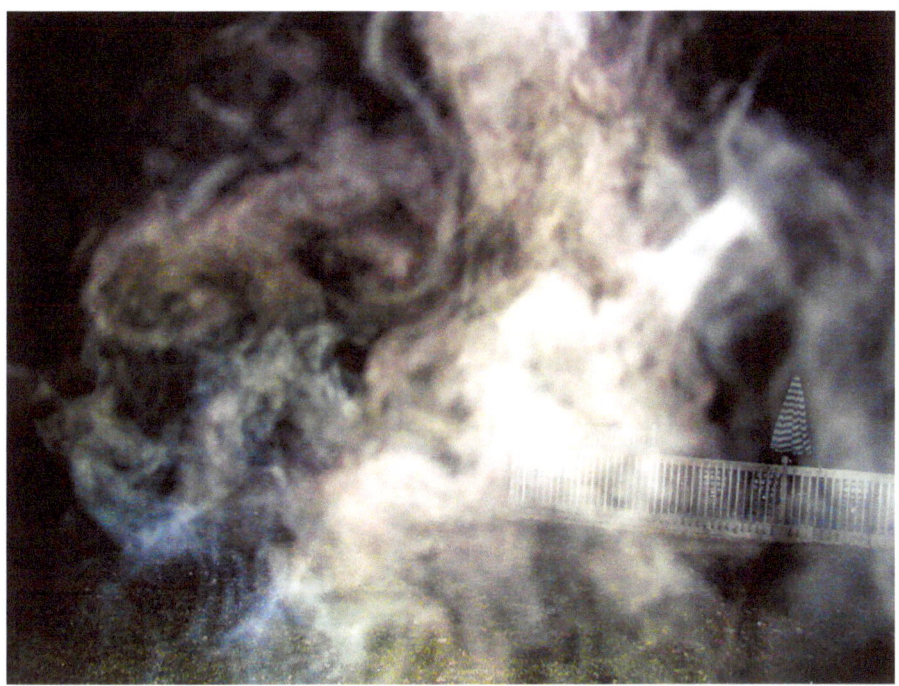

it carries the same gut feeling, the same psychological imprint, and the same comfort level. As I said, it's recognizable, but you have to wait for it to happen, then go outside.

At this point the situation has already changed. Being alone in the dark only enhances one's view of the situation. Things are possible now that aren't possible in the light …crazy things. Sometimes, I imagine that I'm visiting the invisible world that contains those vaporous apparitions and entities, and sometimes, I imagine they are visiting me.

I don't believe the universe works against itself. In other words, if these anomalies were not allowed to be captured in physical form, then we would not be seeing them in these photographs.

Can these experiences be dangerous? I think so, it can be in some cases, especially in the case of a physical apparition. It can be shocking. And that is no BS. It's fkn strange to see this happen. It could affect you physically and/or psychologically. Seeing a pronounced figure appear from thin air and engage you directly may have a lasting effect on your view of reality. Like it or not.

I will admit to witnessing several apparitional occurrences over a period of years, and the only ones that did not immediately scare the living shit out of me, happened so fast, there was no time to be scared. That came after. So if you're still comfortable with this, it's time to step outside ..and wait.

Many thoughts go through your mind when you're alone in the dark. Eventually, you come to realize there are no clear paths to a successful session. I try to disperse the obvious discursions immediately. I usually begin by assessing my safety concerns. After all, I am outside. It is a secluded area but also open to animal intruders, so safety first.

This brings up a thought I entertained at one point, "metal." I became curious as to its impact, if any, on the outcome of the event; rings, eyeglasses, buckles, knives, etc. It's an interesting experiment but its effectiveness proved to be just psychological. At best, I would find metal to be a 50-50 result.

It does afford me the opportunity to discuss knives. I include it as part of my safety program. It's possible my proprietary boundaries may

be broached by animal intruders. Well, that will be a proper mistake for them. These days, I prefer a Tanto blade, but sometimes I still wish for my old Ka-bar.

Don't get me wrong, this option is serious, and I always take it that way. Knives change the situation drastically and should be handled appropriately. After all, this is just a mental exercise, no harm – no foul right? Consider this, you are hopefully about to enter into contact with an anomalous apparition that may look like a goddamn ghost. Why are you carrying a knife? Answer: Respect. Question: Respect for whom? Answer: Yes.

OK, I get it. Warrior culture may be a real thing with them too. How and if that reality unfolds is beyond me. But, it's fun to consider …isn't it?! That's my opinion. This becomes particularly noticeable in the Book of Portraits as the aggressive nature of the imagery is clearly measurable and sometimes disturbingly so.

I believe these are valid considerations, and just because a warrior culture is indicated does not mean we're not friends or allies.

I believe we are. And there is no mistaking my purposeful intentions as directed toward the ancient spirit entity that has appeared. Remember, I'm not the one calling the shots here, I've been called, and I do not believe it was to do me harm.

I have always taken these calls to be friendly. Even though, sometimes friends can be called upon to do strange things. Scary things, like "wanna see what I look like" things. Again, many thoughts go through your mind when you're alone in the dark ...you deal with it. What scares me is their ability to appear instantly out of nowhere, it can be frightening ...and I don't scare easy.

Sadly, I think, it's just outside the reach of human perception and sensibility to confirm there is something sharing our world and it has the ability to appear and disappear at will. Having spent many evenings attempting to engage in new contacts, it would seem to me the will and ability to appear... belongs to them.

Seriously, anything other than a physical appearance is just another story for the campfire. Even still, for credibility sake the appearance of

the anomaly needs to be photographed and authenticated. From the start of this project that has always been my end game; the enigma of spirit photography.

I think after a while the brain runs filters on your thoughts and emotions if any, to decide what to do and when to do it. Click. You begin to develop a thinking style to your mechanics, such as learning to click. I look for conversational thoughts that are out of context, it means something's there …how close is it? I imagine that would be considered instinct. Click.

There is no set of rules or steps to follow that can tell you when to snap the shutter button. The method I follow is basic instinct. I've said before that when engaging in this activity, obviously I think about ghosts and spirits. However, that's not all there is to think about and eventually I'm drawn off to consider other topics.

For instance, I often consider my own mortality. It's easy for that comment to be misinterpreted, it sounds creepy. What I think about is my world - without me in it, and the effect, if any, that might cause.

...a thousand words

It's not creepy, it can be a solemn moment for pause and reflection. During that moment I attempt to view that future world through the eyes of my children. At first I look at my passing in increments of five years, and then ten, twenty, and so on. At times, I feel as though I'm truly there, seeing it unfold in front of me, but not being part of the conversation. In that moment you consider that it's not you invoking the apparition ...you, are the apparition.

I imagine my grandchildren looking through my guitar cases for a new favorite. Or, Thanksgiving and Christmas without grandma and grandpa. Sometimes it sucs; it can be quite sobering, quite sad. Don't get me wrong, I'm also grateful for the opportunity to realize the world that I've known forever is now gone forever and a different world has taken its place. I'm good with that.

I also realize this concept is now an abstract perspective of DNA functionality ...others may disagree.

However, family lines have always been considered to be inherent of genetic tendencies; DNA is what draws them together. It's part of what

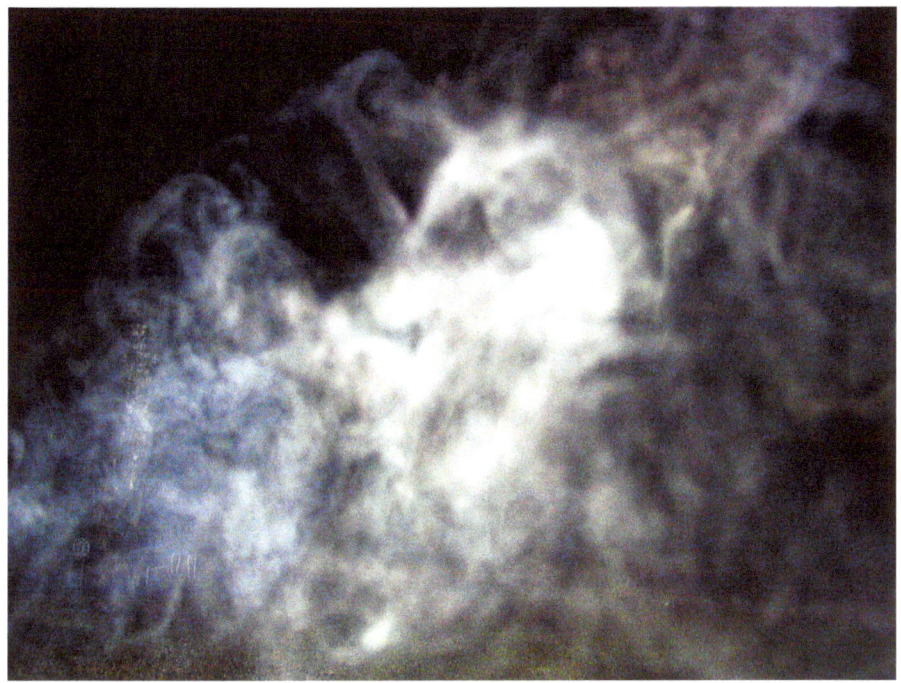

makes them a family. I believe my own descendants will inherit some, all, or combinations of my traits and tendencies, much the same way I've inherited similar contributions from the thousands of ancestors coded into my own DNA.

In my family, I was told my grandmother could see spirits. No other family member was accused of having this talent. Interestingly, based on my DNA tests results, my grandmother would have registered at approximately 80% Native American. It's the old blood …Beringian.

For me it answers a few questions, such as an admiration for knives and weapons, a love of open flame cooking, and my belief in the spirits. Instances like those are common, however, when you consider them as ancestral spirit connections and there's a twinkle of truth involved, it can be quite comforting. I've learned much since my DNA test.

I wonder if it's why sometimes I think they can read your mind. If one imagines the phenomenon initiates from within, and then exteriorized due to some force mechanism, then yeah, it's reasonable to think they can read your mind.

It's also reasonable to assume the exteriorized force is a reflection of an underlying subconscious ancestral personality, with a mind of its own, having once imagined its own mortality.

At times I feel responsible to share facts as I know them, opinions as I think them, and truths as I hold them. Privacy has always been a major concern for me. After all, we are talking about spirit communication, ghost sightings and supernatural occurrences.

It's weird, no doubt about it. Do I want to be the weirdo shooting photographs in my backyard in the dark at 2:00 am? Fk no. But I did it anyway. Honestly, privacy has always been a concern to me. It's one of the reasons I haven't engaged in publishing a complete history of my work, until now.

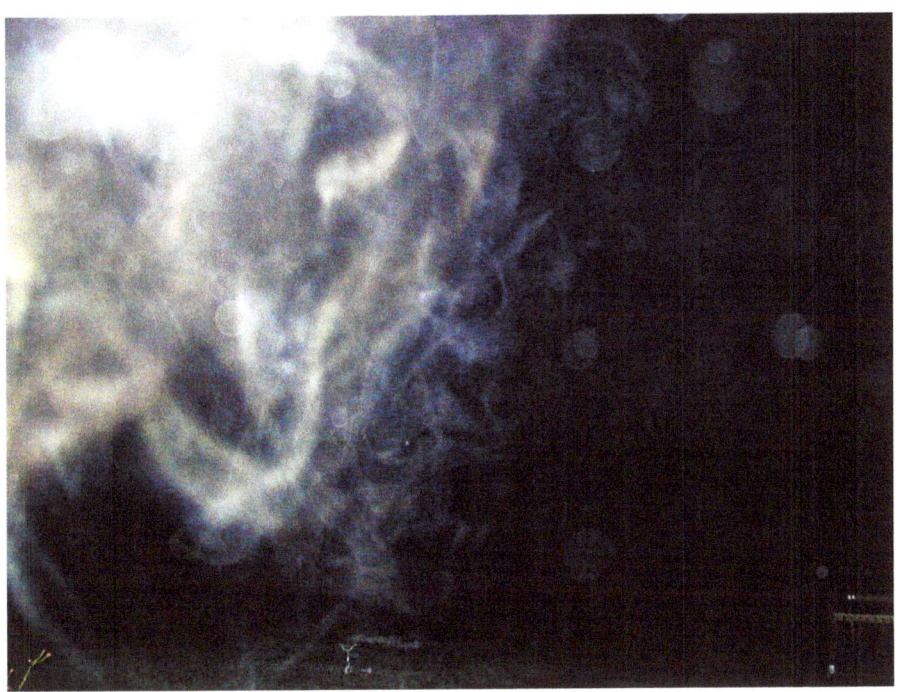

THE OTHER SIDE OF THE LENS
ectoplasm: theory of emanations

Under the circumstances we have an opportunity to explore this phenomenon of unusual apparitions closely. We have the data. And amongst other things we can use this data to contemplate scenarios that offer answers / solutions / ideas. Firstly, we are dealing with a recurring phenomenon - Anomalous Apparitions.

There are times when I believe I'm reading my own reflection. It's a feeling I have now and then. I find it very interesting. I also find it very difficult to dismiss, it's an obvious explanation. The common factor is the other side of the lens.

Is this Ectoplasm? Perhaps, that is one possibility, though ectoplasm remains scientifically unproven to exist …others may disagree. Another possibility is a wandering spirit, but …same problem.

So perhaps it's nothing at all. Interestingly, nothing at all, would be misleading and the least serious conclusion, but feel free.

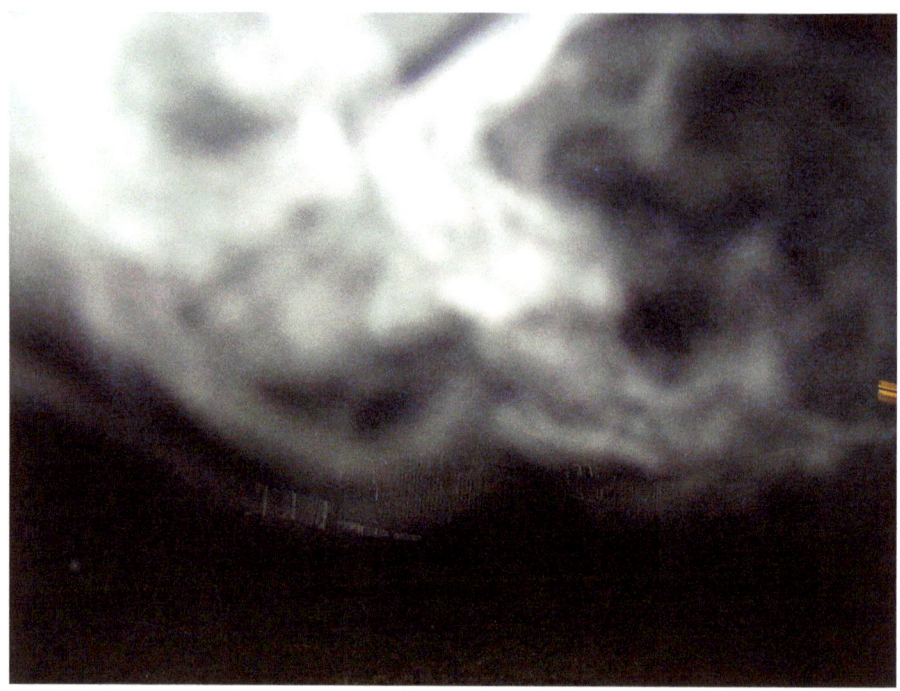

Ectoplasmic concepts and external interactions can be simultaneous events. Reasoning can be developed to account for both to engage within the shared space area for various purposes. It's the physical formation called into question on these events as well as the origin of the anomaly.

Supernatural theories that confidently rely on visual aids are rare, legitimate visual aides are unusually rare. However, visuals are helpful to understanding what may be taking place during an event. If indeed, information has been recorded that is helpful in understanding, or just glimpsing a supernatural event as a point of human interest, then I think it should be shared as such. So be it.

I too, am a fan of supernatural phenomena, have been since I'm a kid. I've never seen anything like this …ever. It's one of the reasons I'm sharing. There are other reasons, but, if I don't share this as is then you'd never know this happened in the manner in which it did. I believe that's reason enough to share. If it were me, I'd want to know the facts.

In this case we are in a unique position of having access to all known participating elements to examine and scrutinize for answers, ideas and concepts; the primary (photographer), the subject (apparition), and the original location (property). I see this as a rare opportunity to explore the anomalous apparition phenomenon.

While viewing the subject (apparition), it's easy to focus one's direct attention on the anomaly as the source of the occurrence. But, when you realize your focus may be biased via the lens, re-focusing to observe a wider field of vision introduces a new element …it's the other side of the lens. Both elements are now part of the bigger picture within an objective field. This means more data from an alternate perspective.

This exercise is revealing. Focus often falls on the reflective image (the anomaly) even though the origin and purpose of the anomaly is considered to be unknown. Now there's the human element included as well, (the other side of the lens) and the origin and purpose of the anomaly is still considered to be unknown. I wonder why?

It does give cause to consider an objective field or a "zone" may at times contain the necessary elements to achieve positive outcomes. One could assume the source of the anomalous event is present when using these common field parameters and boundaries.

This also now opens the gate for ectoplasm theory. The applied term "ectoplasm" was started by a renowned Nobel Prize laureate in 1894: "[...] a substance or spiritual energy 'exteriorized' by physical mediums." Is that a real thing? So far, science says no. What I see appears to support historical superstitious concepts of ectoplasm theory. Having considered this at length, I imagine a realistic concept is possible if you include the DNA factor. It's a clean, realistic and logical approach to making sense of a lesser understood phenomenon.

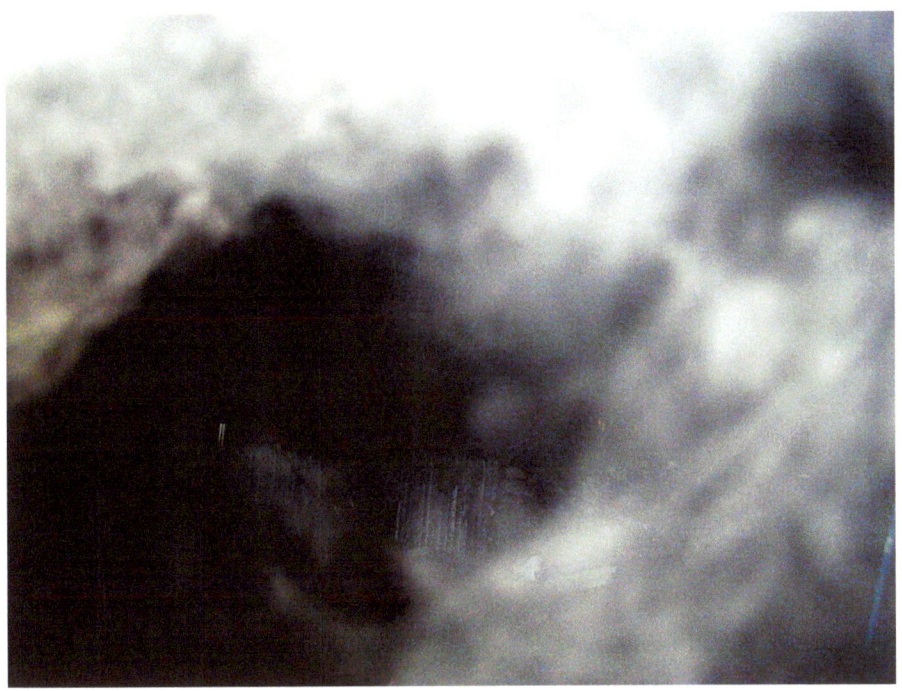

DNA Factor

DNA factors provide support for dynamic and unique apparitional occurrences. What makes sense to me, particularly, is if/when the event (exteriorized substance) is relegated to or through the presence of the medium (whatever). The substance from that individual is likely going to include the proprietary DNA of that individual. That's just fkn science.

That DNA contribution constitutes a lone identity, I like that. It makes a lot of sense. It indicates that an ancestral spirit connection is possible and can go back in time thousands of years.

Combining both ectoplasm theory and DNA factors is an excellent solution when addressing the concept of ancestral spirit connections. Sometimes, when I'm reviewing the photographs and images, I consider the results of my own DNA test, and my known and newly discovered ancestral locations. For example, it impacted the way I watched television. Having always been a fan of Westerns, I always liked some of the Indians, now I know why.

To be clear, we are speaking of genetic ancestral properties present in an individual's DNA, the ancestral qualities; the mystery, the history, of us all. But whatever test results my DNA may ultimately return, I will always claim 100% red blooded USA American, born on Long Island, New York, in the year of our Lord 1960 ...yeah, I'm gettin' up there.

When speaking of ancestral influences, it should not be overlooked some were inhabitants of civilizations no longer in existence. But, the DNA of that ancestral experience is alive in one's own body. The full depth of DNA is still being explored by genetic scientists, and a determination of ancestral genetic connections has been firmly established for many years.

That being said, my DNA results are more than satisfying to my ambitions. My two primary DNA percentages are of Sicilian and Native American heritage. To that I say "fkn a", couldn't be happier. Two of my absolute favorite cultures, now I know why. These two DNA factors combine for nearly 75% of my total DNA.

My indigenous DNA indicates Beringian ancestry, a land bridge crosser, a hunter, an explorer, and one of the four founding Native American DNA groups. My haplogroup match (single common ancestor) has been recovered from a skeleton in North America dating back almost 13,000 years.

Fk the Mayflower. JK

I had no idea there was Native blood. I'm raised New York Italian. And, to make it more interesting, my remaining results indicate an overwhelming variety of worldwide cultures and civilizations, including: Iberian, Egyptian, Arabian, Ashkenazi, North and Sub-Saharan African, Caucasus, Levant and Mesopotamia. That's a lot to think about. Imagine the position this puts me in.

Singular results range between .5% and 55%. Considering even .1% indicates a distant ancestral figure, how can you discount it? You can't. And to be clear, when discussing ancestral DNA, we are determining a single common ancestor, potentially dating back thousands of years. It's interesting to think about.

Along the way, there are literally thousands of ancestors you have descended from that have left an impact on your DNA. Considering DNA factors along with ectoplasm theory in general is no crazier than ectoplasm theory alone.

As I've said, I have often looked at my photos and images in an effort to reveal a possible connection with an ancestral spirit entity. At times, I believe, I find them. It's a personal project of mine and could result in a reasonable spirit interpretation with my ancestral past. And I do find that very interesting.

If in fact ectoplasm theory is a real thing, DNA factors are obviously connected, to what extent is to be determined. Others may disagree with this concept. Ectoplasm has not been substantiated scientifically. Therefore, it does not exist. And there is no reason to assume that DNA is a mitigating factor, until now. That's my opinion. Granted, we're in some thin line territory here, but in my book, it makes sense.

Consider for a moment spirit research and the discourse that often surrounds it. The objective for much of what has been presented thus far is communication with the souls of the dead. I believe many things possible, but it's not for me to decide what the anomalies truly represent …it's just to represent them truly.

Apparitions are an incredibly rare phenomenon. I contemplate the reactions of others, not only the so called experts in the field, but everyday people who have an interest in this field.

Are these the remnants of dead people? I can't answer that. If I were to render my best guess, based on the photographic evidence, I imagine them as an intelligent species of natural origin. There's no evidence to indicate these anomalies ever occupied the bodies of human beings even though at times recognizable features are obvious.

Alternatively what we are witnessing is a species of intelligent semi invisible beings occupying the same space considered to be the domain of the spiritual afterlife. Under the circumstances, one can imagine the confusion. However, it does appear to be a logical conclusion.

...a thousand words

To be clear, I don't know how it works, what they are, or where they come from. I'm guessing, but I'm using accurate and substantial data to reasonably assume a working hypothesis. Like I said, we are in some thin line territory here, but it works for me. It's a lot to imagine at first, and a bit overwhelming, but ectoplasm theory combined with DNA factors offers a reasonable and objective conclusion. Others may disagree.

*"...these images may reflect the influence
of the original supernatural occurrence that created them."*

Portraits 3.1

Book of Portraits

Book of Portraits

Portraits are supernatural illusions. They are a visual interpretation of the persona of a captured spirit …in detail. Yes, I said captured spirit. The silence is deafening, but I hear what you're thinking; bullshit. OK, then that's where we should begin.

Tell me, what part of the prior chapter on "Apparitions" did you not understand? A Portrait begins with a single untouched photograph of an apparition, or in other words, a "captured spirit"; my data source.

I've named one of the Portraits "James" after myself. He is an image projected from my own psychosis. As such, I've been able to see past the pretense of good or evil in favor of a more stimulating concept; a subliminal spirit influence, or, a complex spirit interpretation. Let's discuss…

I believe the supernatural effect of the original spirit occurrence may remain as part of the reflective image. The effect, intentional or otherwise may be useful as a vehicle for subliminal influences. That may sound disturbing, but it's exactly what we're looking for.

Wouldn't it be interesting if the influence is intended to be reflected on sight? Is that a problem, I hope not. Nothing indicating harm, psychological or otherwise is intended. But proceed with caution. We're dealing with a rare unconfirmed event. It may be supernatural.

Over the years I've attempted to associate the presumed influence a particular Portrait might inspire and why. A successful exercise sometimes resulted in the naming of a Portrait, though not always. It's difficult to understand when you don't speak the language.

The Book of Portraits is an accounting of the exploration and the recovery of anomalous supernatural entities I captured under the terms and conditions of darkness. No one is more bewildered than I. You should believe that. Whatever I was doing, whatever I was thinking, it worked. How do you think that makes me feel? You must decide for yourself. And I agree. I realize this sounds crazy, I'm dealing with it, so should you.

I found them by using a computer and utilizing what I call a "touch sensitive" method of extraction to transform an anomalous photograph into a Portrait. It's a method that removes obstructions to reveal a detailed anomalous presence. I will demonstrate.

The process I use requires a computer, a digital tablet and pen, and an image processing program to complete the transformations. Yes, I touched these images. Yes, I realize that ...it's kind of the point.

It's interesting to note the unique personalities of each Portrait, and yet, they all suffered the same mechanics from start to finish. The surface material, the lighting, the hot-spots, most have eyes, some have teeth… details vary from subject to subject; however, they all remain similar in composition as well as being unique. Just like us.

Parallel development systems should not be an uncommon question. A unique entity, such as us, requires rules that render us unique. Those rules are DNA. Parallel rules, or a set thereof being applied during the development process of other unique anomalous entities is a reasonable assumption. This becomes an interesting concept as rules infer authority, and authority infers hierarchy, and hierarchies infer an organized and systematic intelligence. Just like us.

This concept gave cause to consider the earlier claim; "they are as individually unique in their race, as we are within our own." I have to believe that. You can decide for yourself.

There is much more to see when you look closely. For instance, the nested personalities or the illusion that is revealed within some of the Portraits stretch the limits of the human imagination. I consider those illusions examples of pure awesomeness and the rest as simply incredible. That's my opinion, and while I certainly stand in awe of these illusionary images, admittedly, I have no direct answer for this phenomenon.

Honestly, I believe the level of supernatural involvement is at an immeasurable state. Therefore, I cannot confirm or deny the intended objective(s) of the anomaly or the source that produced it …nor can anyone else. This refers to the psychological effects and/or the physical confrontations. And that's the dilemma each and every time.

The cause for concern, if any, is the influence cannot be immediately measured as being a sublime, malevolent or mundane experience. I have struggled with this for many years. At first, the presumed influence of a Portrait may appear to be obvious. I have found that is not usually the case, they are dynamic, unrealized supernatural forces with an objective.

The influence may be a sudden inspiration of confidence, or caution, anger or rage, it's that thought that came out of nowhere, some say Muse, some say Sage. On the other hand, it could be rendered subtly, unbeknown to the recipient. It lingers within, potentially forming an unconscious psychic bias or awareness, it depends how you look at it.

I'm confident these influences are responsible for the apparitions and the inspiration for the Book of Portraits. There's just too many of them to be an accident. This concept is a rigorous one as it would require the status of unique spiritual entities capable of directing or influencing thought, actions and/or behavior, I just hold the camera.

Of course that may be my imagination running wild or it may be a cautionary warning, it's also possible it's where we're headed. It's the main reason I share cautionary warnings about this material …because results matter.

I believe my part to play is to provide accurate information that will allow you to proceed with a reserved confidence in its authenticity and effectiveness as a unique supernatural illusion.

Some may choose to engage the Portraits in a semi-meditative state in an effort to enhance the spiritual experience, they are after all, supernatural images. In such cases, determining the effectiveness of a Portrait as an influential resource is and should be the determined wish and responsibility of the observer.

Making a connection with a Portrait is for you to decide. One might ask, "why would I want to make a connection?" The purpose of that is for you to determine. I only represent the Portraits are the derived results of apparitions that were photographed during random states of a physical materialization, that in and of itself should be cause for concern.

Further concern regarding influences may or may not be justified if and until it's determined that subliminals are possible. Can they act as an active force capable of propelling thoughts upon a secondary target? Is that even possible? I would have to say, yes, I think it's very possible. Furthermore, the evidence indicates the influence is an active force even before the apparition is captured.

So when did it begin? And when did it end? I've often considered the possibility I am being tricked into first capturing and subsequently releasing these images to the public as a sinister means of allowing them to acquire subliminal access to this slice of reality.

If indeed that turns out to be true, then all I can say is, "Whoa to you, for this day has been brought forth for reasons known only to them. …stand very still and deal with it."

Determination of earthly Evil is an easy tell, contemplating the determination of supernatural Evil …not so easy.

Historically, warnings have been given to be on the lookout for deception, trickery and lies. Flatly stated, I don't believe you can out-think an ancient spirit with an agenda. A good example of a lie, trick or deception …is when you think you can.

Remember what we agreed to, mental exercises, no harm – no foul. However, I do believe a cause for concern is justified. My estimation may seem harsh, but I think one should double down with confidence that we are in witness of a rare supernatural phenomenon.

One cannot dismiss the fact that several hundred or even several thousand years of civil education, science, and various technologies have been administered alongside a steady diet of legends, superstitions, and ancestral teachings that are woven into the fabric of modern reality. The fact that we are now dealing with hi-definition photographic images and digital technology makes this a very interesting phenomenon, and one that proves difficult to dismiss. The similarities of historical descriptions and narratives are at last revealed and presented to a modern mind.

In order to approach this concept with any chance of serious consideration, the evidence supporting a righteous conclusion is the only objective. First, let's determine the abstract physical attributes of the supernatural entities portrayed in books of the old and new testaments of the Bible, and the images in the Book of Portraits. The results may be a startling cause for concern …that's my opinion.

Do these images portray entities with wings? Do these images portray entities with horns? Do these images portray entities with eyes? Do these images portray entities with teeth? Do these images portray entities with multiple heads? The answer is of course, yes.

One cannot help but notice similarities analogous to historical descriptions of the supernatural beings in the Book of Daniel, Ezekiel, or Revelation. But this time, they're not drawings or paintings, they're photographic captures, and that changes everything.

Consider this, if the entities portrayed in this work are in fact supernatural entities of angelic or demonic origin, are they the same supernatural entities that have existed since time began? That's a scary thought, because it could be true.

Still interested? It's not too late. You can still turn back. You can close this book and step away. Agreed?

Rule #1: Don't shoot the messenger.

Rule #2: Don't shoot the fkn messenger.

I'm relieved and honored the class of entity I encountered, was intelligent and very cool about it. It makes me wonder, as I often do, about the psychological effects supernatural reflective imagery imposes on the viewer, intentional or otherwise.

I also think seeing how the original photographs transform into a Portrait should either put your mind at ease, or frighten you. Either way, no one is trying to trick you. There is no need for that. Portraits are an extraordinary phenomenon that invokes a simple reality, and reveals a rare and unusual occurrence.

Considering the detail and realism of the Portraits, a determination of intelligence becomes convincingly acceptable. Seeing the anatomical similarities of bilaterally symmetrical characters, or the abundance of strikingly unique personalities, it's not hard to imagine a supernatural force is at hand.

The problem, if any, is in overcoming a predetermined concept of what a supernatural event is, and who's performing it.

I am convinced these occurrences are supernatural in effect, and I do not want to be responsible for the intentions of someone other than myself during this process. No offense, but I trust myself to be fair and reasonable in my determinations, and by this time so should you.

Attempting to dismiss these occurrences as coincidental may prove to be challenging. On the other hand, one might also agree with an assessment of coincidental if the occurrences were limited in scope to one or two incidents.

...a thousand words

However, what if there were 10 incidents, or 20, or 30, or 50, or 100? Clearly, a more discerning effort is necessary to confront the challenges that are reflective of their true nature. Accordingly, this phenomenon is firmly addressable as an intellectual challenge.

For instance, consider the photo in *Figure (TB1)*. It appears to be an unremarkable semi-transparent form resembling smoke, mist, or vapor, on a dark background. That's a fair and reasonable observation. Stating this photo is one of the anomalous images captured during my nighttime photo sessions is irrelevant, it's still an unremarkable photograph.

Supernaturalism is not magic, it says so right in the name, "natural" ...and I agree. However, super-nature and the effects surrounding it, including anomalous apparitions, may appear to some as being magical. I can assure you it's not the case.

The photograph in *Figure (TB1)* illustrates a useful mechanism of natural deception. The alleged entity is hiding in plain sight.

Sadly, there is no way for me to prove this is a naturally occurring phenomenon of super-nature, and that's why I call them illusions... supernatural illusions.

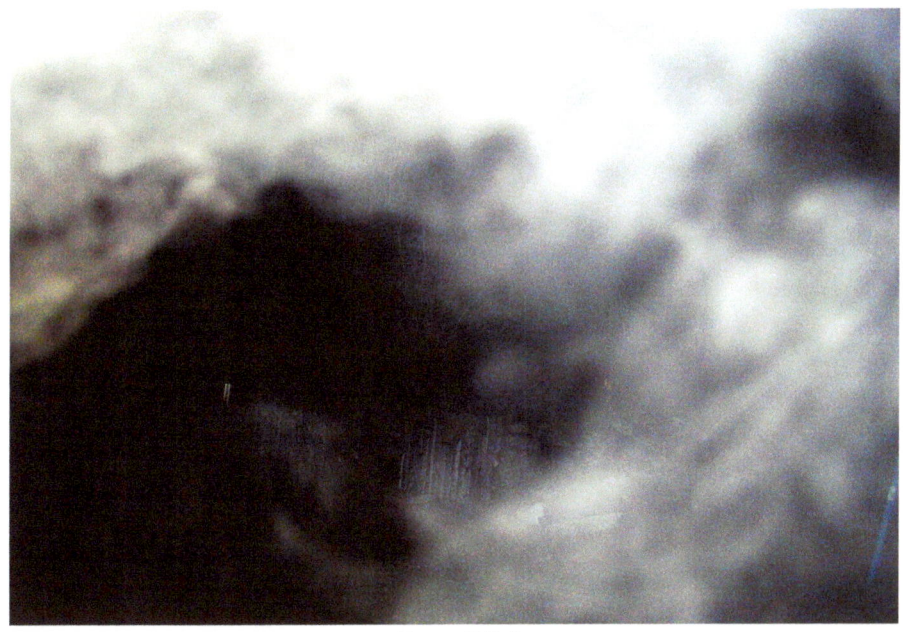

Figure (TB1)

This collection of Portraits contains twenty six original images. All Portraits are developed from a single photograph of an anomalous apparition. All apparition photographs were shot by JD. All Portrait names have been applied cautiously, thoughtfully, and respectably in accordance with their unique mystical appearance. These images may reflect a supernatural origin, that's all I can say.

WINGS OF THE WIND

...a thousand words

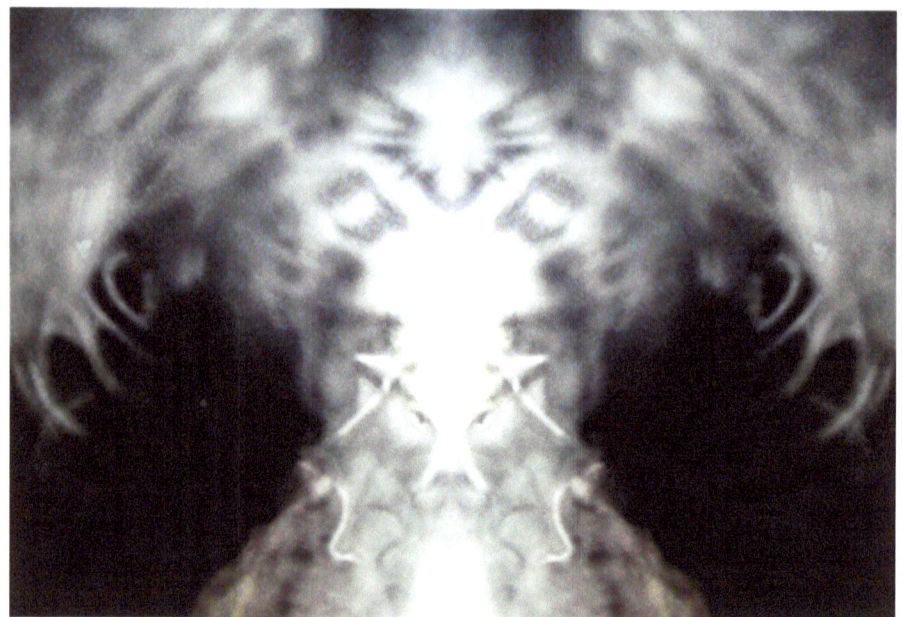

T-Bone

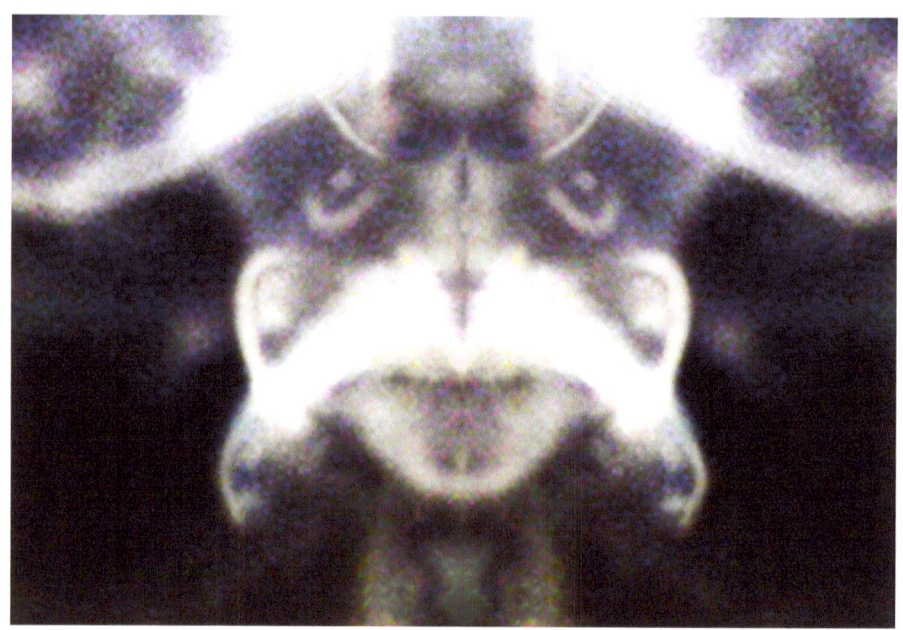

Wyatt

...a thousand words

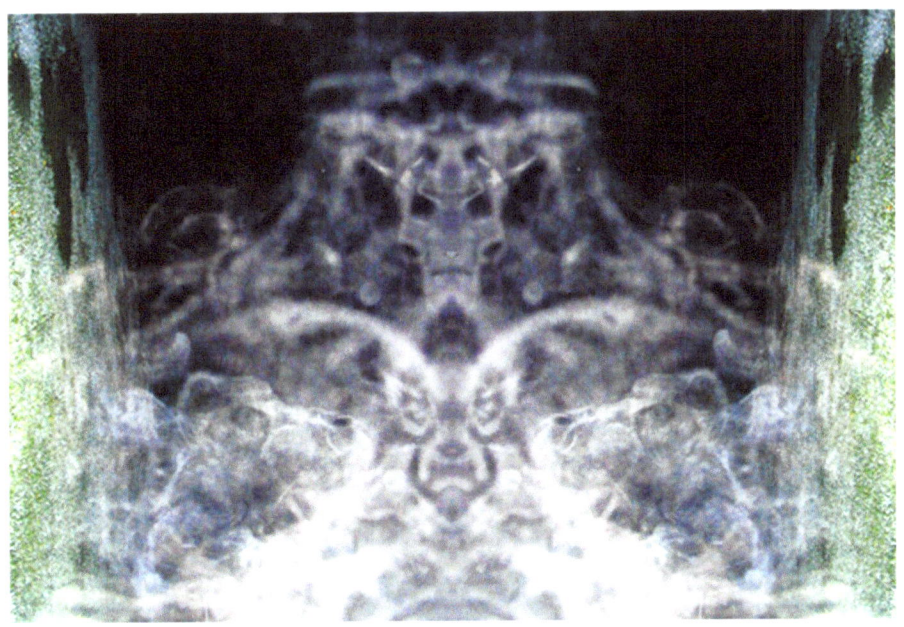

Fingers

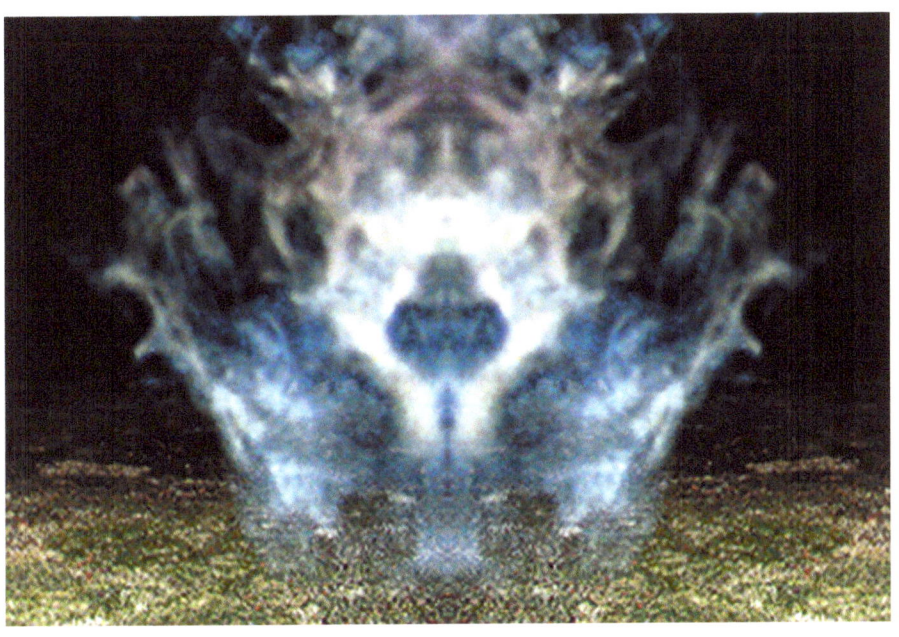

King Dragon

...a thousand words

JAMES

CHIEF

...a thousand words

LORD OF THE SEVEN DAYS

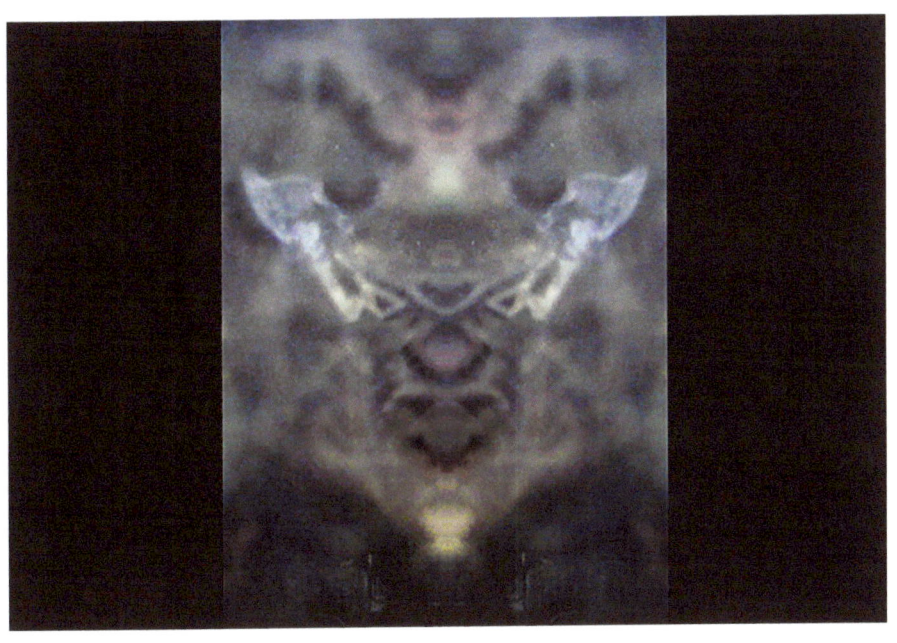

BEAST OF THE ANGELS

...a thousand words

DJRA-KUL-A-DIN

SPIRIT OF THE SECOND SIGHT

...a thousand words

HAMMERHEAD

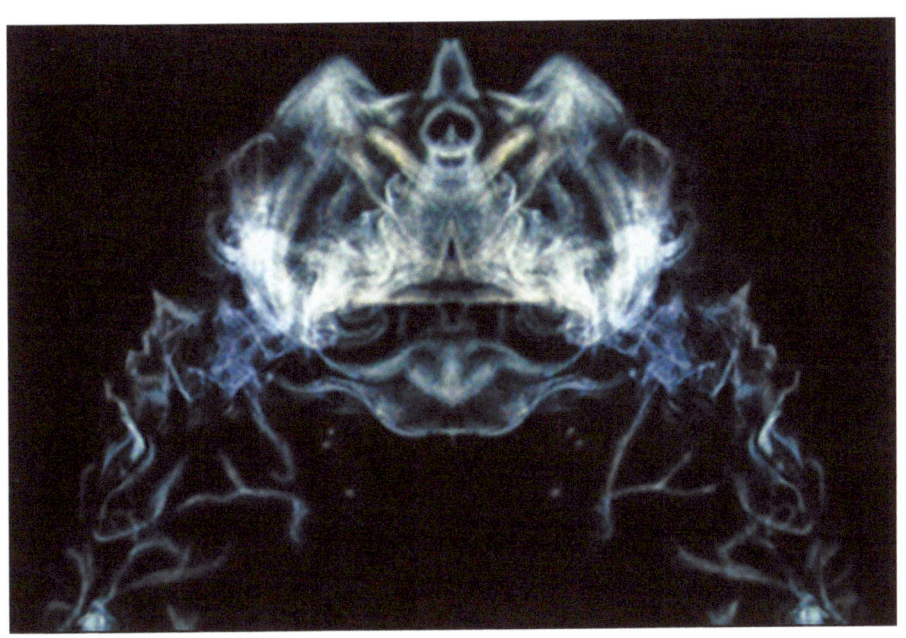

FLAG

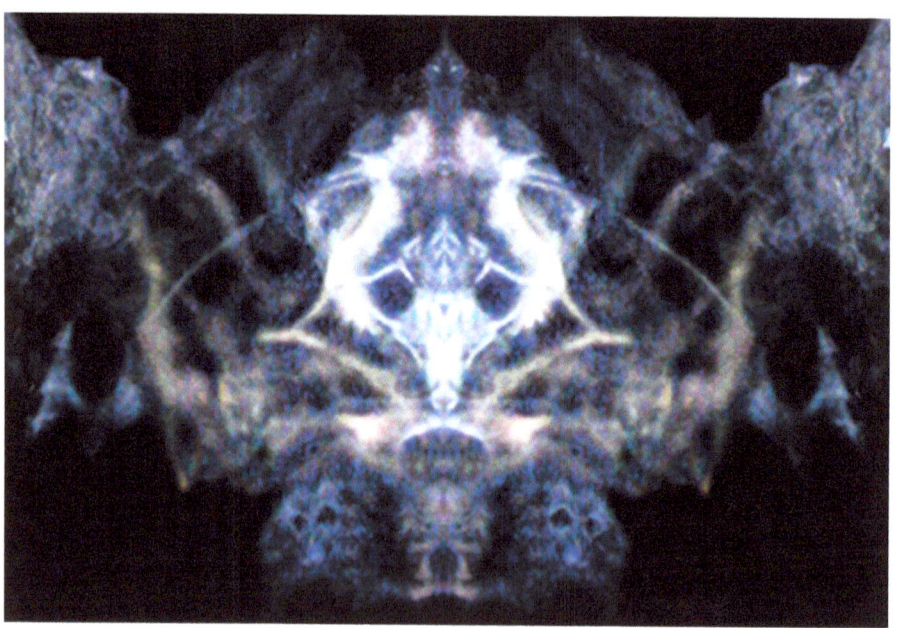

Fang

ChilliPop

…a thousand words

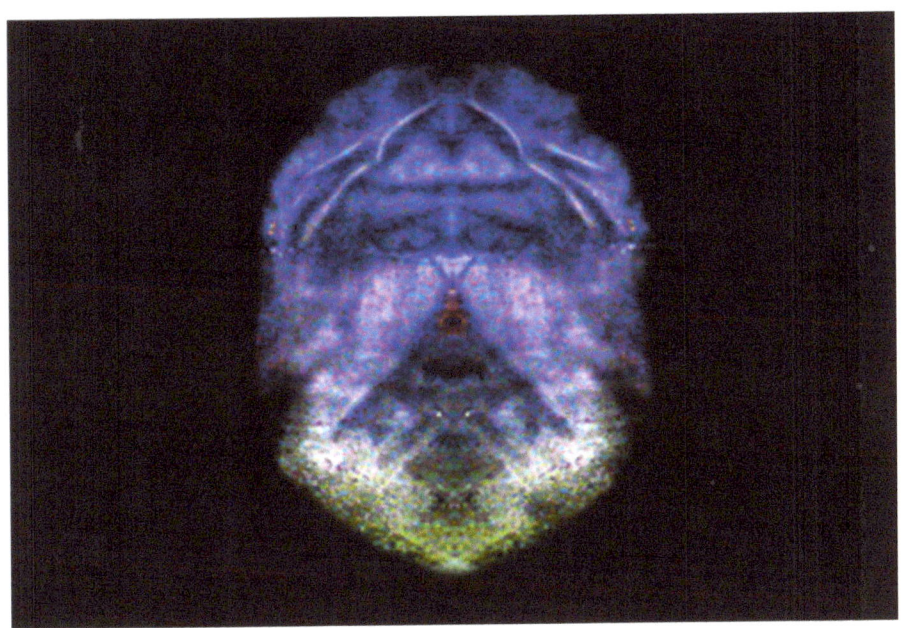

Instant Karma

Dr. Seven

...a thousand words

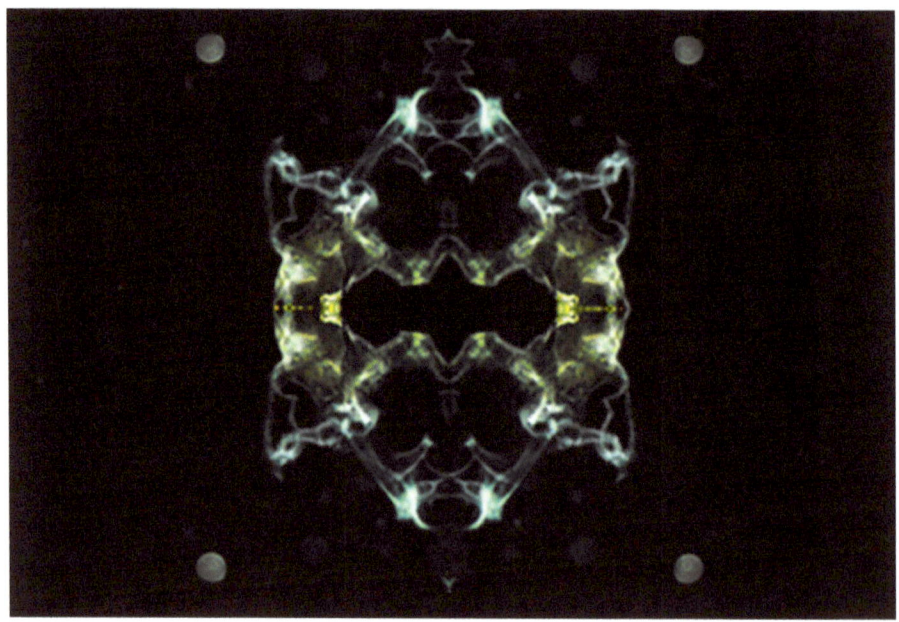

Karats

Endora

...a thousand words

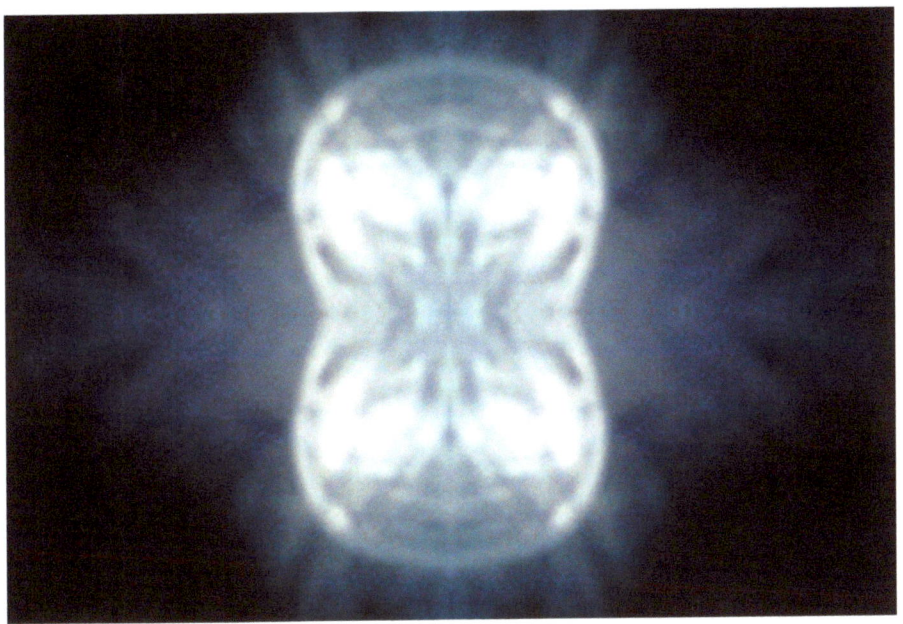

THE DRIP

SPARX

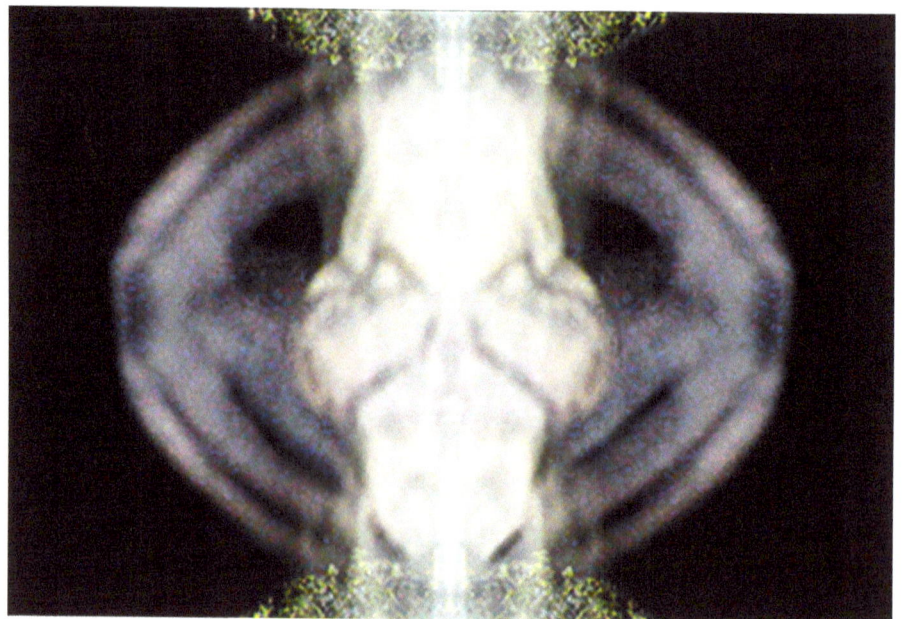

Aquadio

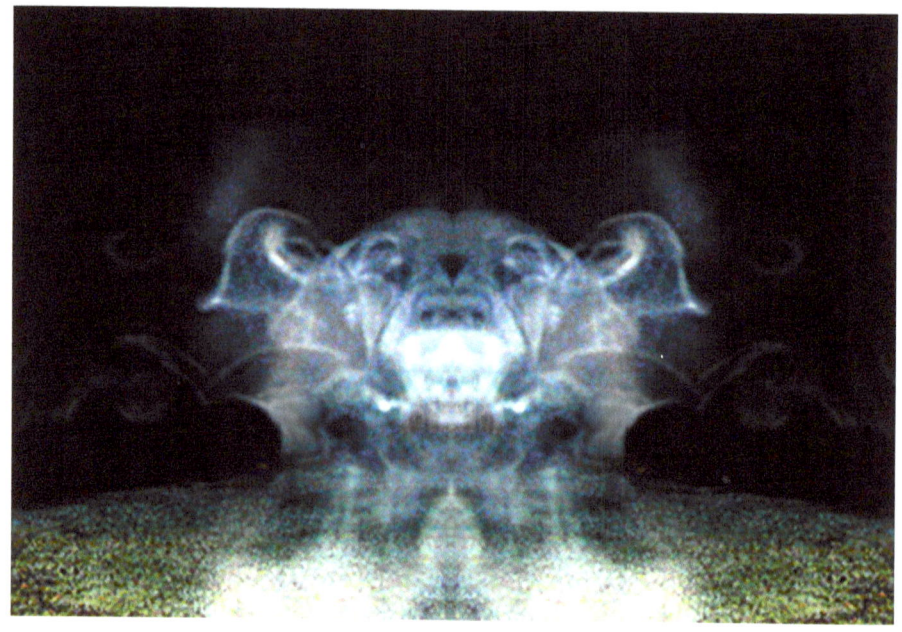

Prince Dragon

...a thousand words

JOHN THE ELDER

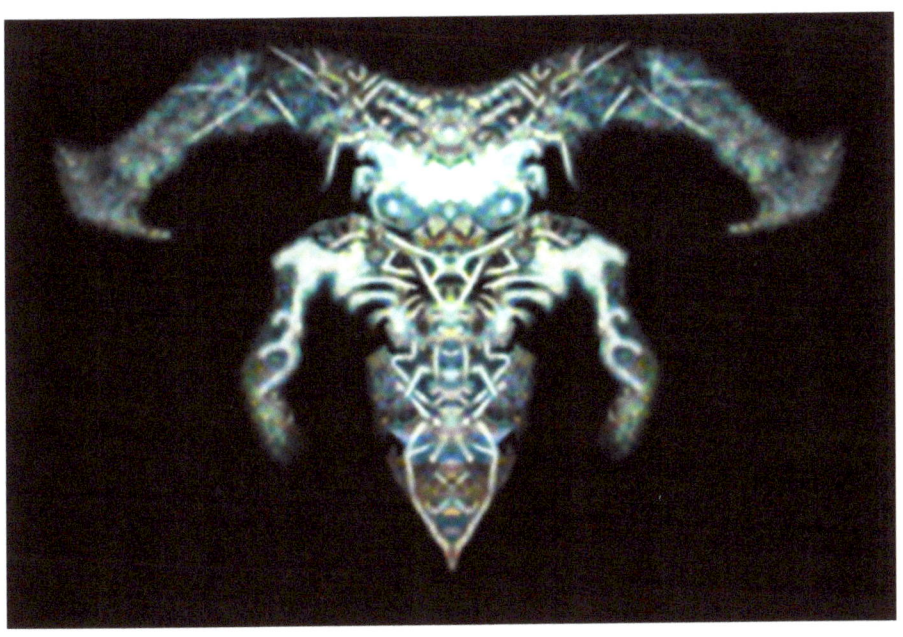

ACE

Bones

When considering the Portraits as representative of supernatural deities, at times one must also take into consideration the spectrum of good and evil. The collection of deities in the Book of Portraits appears to embrace the concept that a wide range of personalities are represented, however, the determination an image is representative of a good spirit or an evil spirit has no basis in fact and is left up to the discretion of the observer.

...the author

...a thousand words

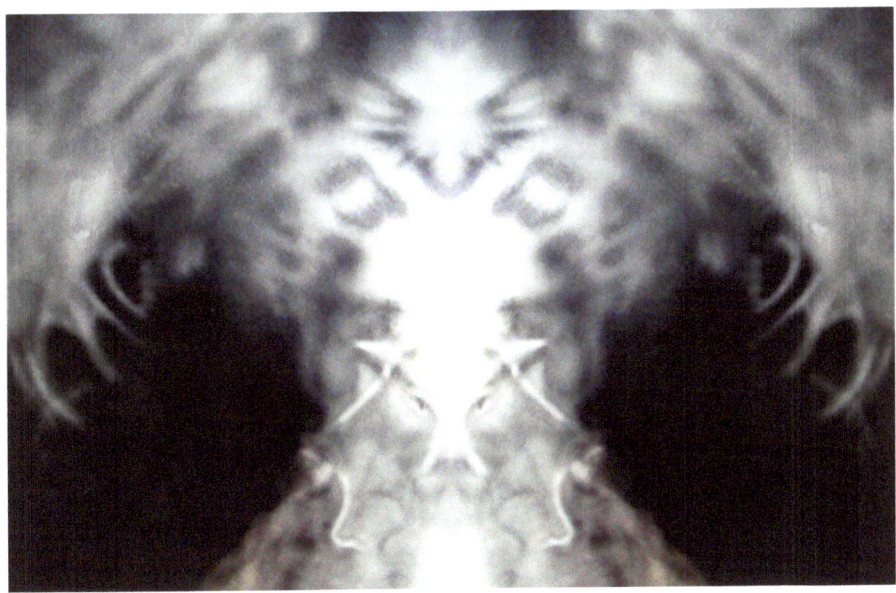

T-Bone
Angel of the Dead and Buried
Portrait by JD

This Portrait epitomizes the enigma of a supernatural phenomenon. How does one reconcile the distinct representation of a winged canine? Difficulties arise when trying to fit this into a common natural reality, accordingly, I refer to them as Illusions.

Portraits are created by using a single photograph of a previously captured anomalous apparition. Often, the original perspective of the image in the photograph is challenging, and difficult to determine if an intelligent personality is hidden within; therefore, adjustments are applied in various sequences in order to locate the anomaly if one exists ...such as this one.

Once an anomaly is identified, an effort is undertaken to enhance the details of the underlying features. Protecting the integrity of the original image is necessary in order to render an accurate interpretation of its personality. I've included this Portrait and subsequent images as an example of the methodologies I might employ, so you can see what I see… and why I call them Supernatural Illusions.

...a thousand words

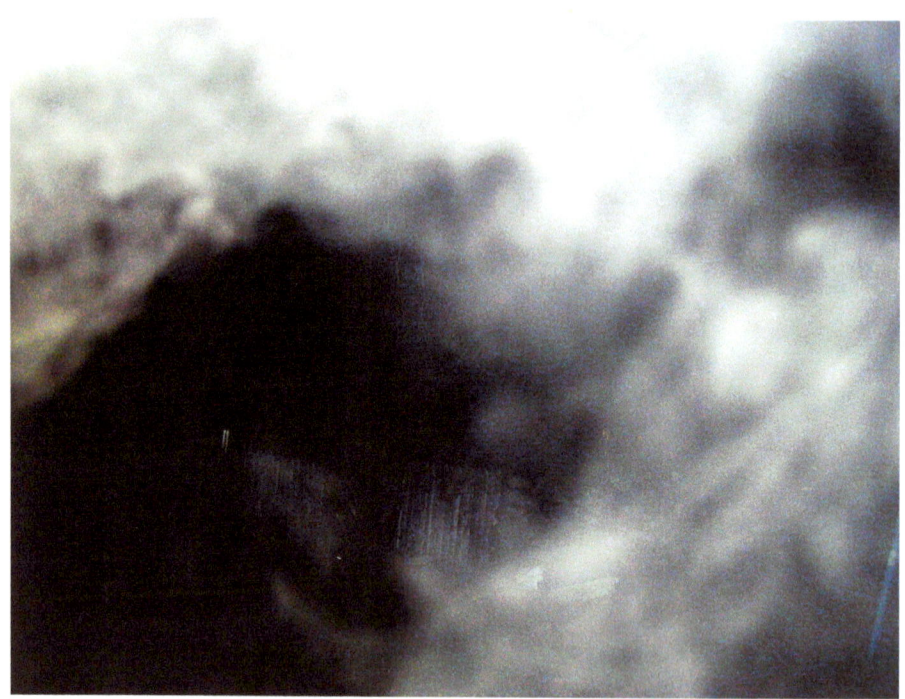

T-bone (1) - original photo - Figure (TB1)

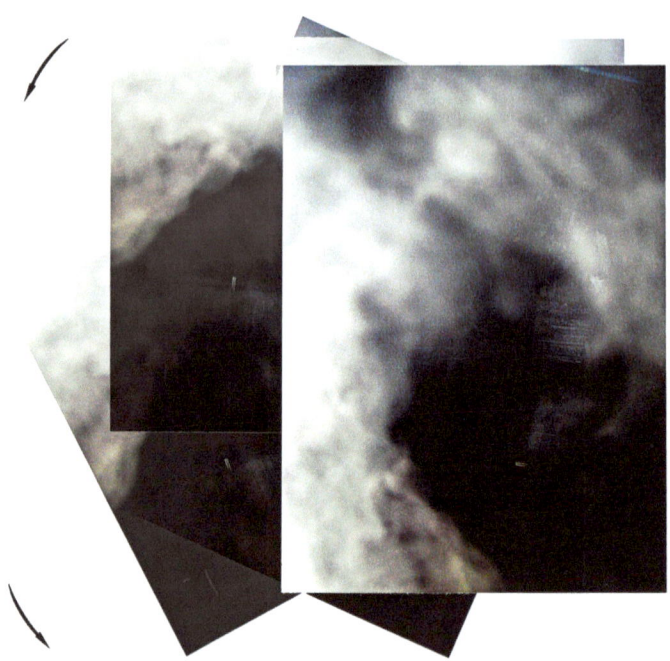

T-bone (2) - original photo - rotate to 90° CCW

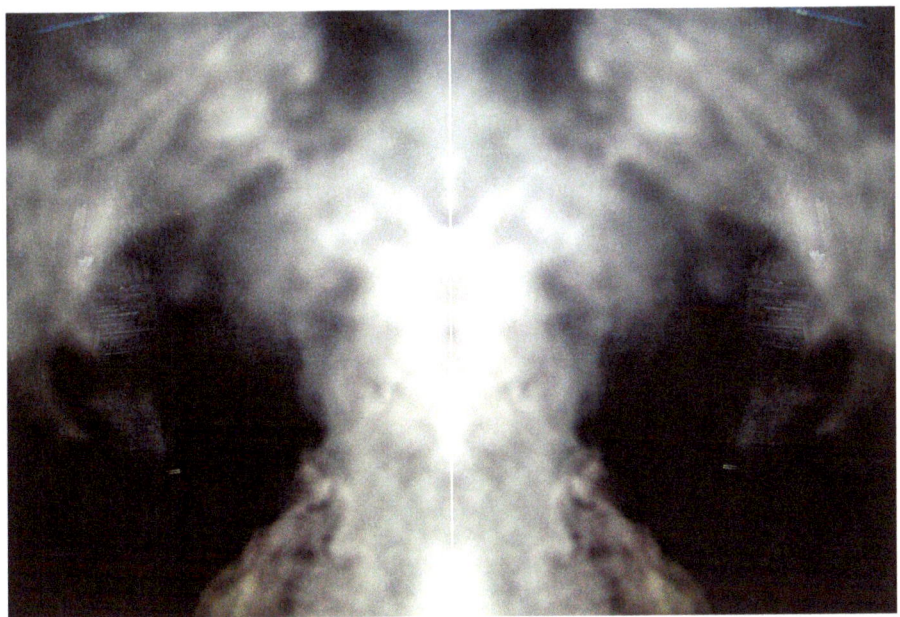

T-bone (3) - (R) original rotated 90° CCW - (L) mirrored image

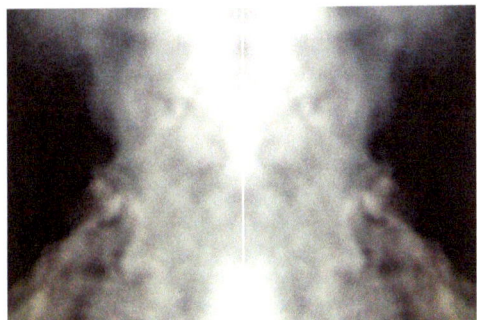

T-bone (4) – pre-extraction

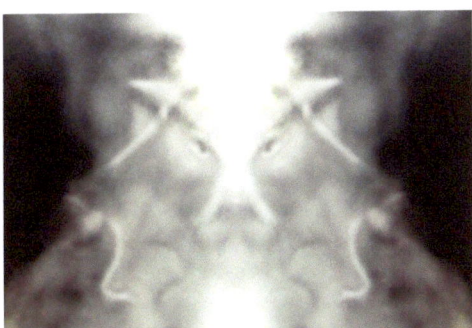

T-bone (5)

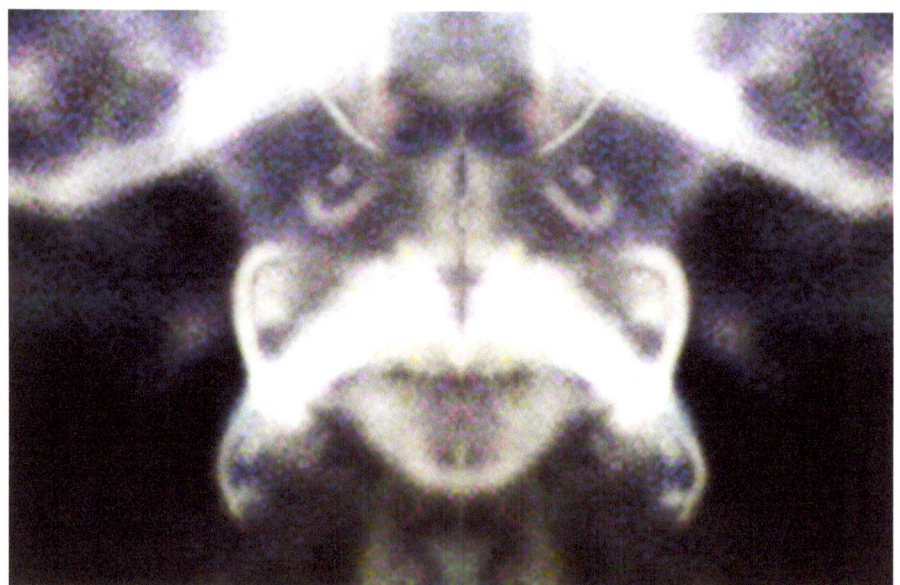

WYATT

Portrait by JD

Meet Wyatt, I find the realism of Wyatt comfortably disturbing. As you can see, the apparition in Wyatt's original photograph is in very close proximity to the camera lens, they can get very close, very quickly. I have usually found that to be a very good sign, it means there's activity coming from a strong and determined source.

In some cases, a basic global adjustment of the image reveals a high percentage of the personality that was previously unnoticed. In other cases, a hands-on approach is necessary. And finally, not all photographs result in a positive Portrait. In Wyatt's case, a strong foundation for a new Portrait is obvious.

Wyatt is an apparition. He literally existed for less than one second. But he displays a seriously complex and sympathetic anatomy. He gives the impression that he can see you. When you look at him you say, "Hey Wyatt", to yourself as if he was really there. Is Wyatt is a ghost? No. It's an illusion. The Portraits are created from the appearance of a ghost, spirit or presence. Once you see their faces it's easier to accept them as a supernatural anomaly …an intelligent supernatural anomaly.

Wyatt (1) - original photo

The night I shot Wyatt, it was a startling but comfortable sighting; it was like Boom, in your face. He was so fkn close to me, that's the crazy part, it happens so fast and they can be right up on you. I saw him looking at me; seeing a face or part of the face makes it personal for me, somehow you seem to think they were being friendly. It might just be wishful thinking on my part, that they wanted to be friends, but you know what, if wishful thinking is what it takes to get it done and come out of it intact, then I guess I'm just a wishful thinker.

Notice Wyatt appears to have a "film" around him, it's a soft type of blurriness, and many, but not all of the apparitions have this "film." One thought would be it's due to the speed at which the apparitions appear, the camera lens does not have enough time to properly refocus on the occurrence. Also, the apparitions are not still when they appear, they are in motion, sometimes subtly and sometimes abruptly. It's difficult to describe but I have also seen movement within the apparition itself almost like blood moving through veins.

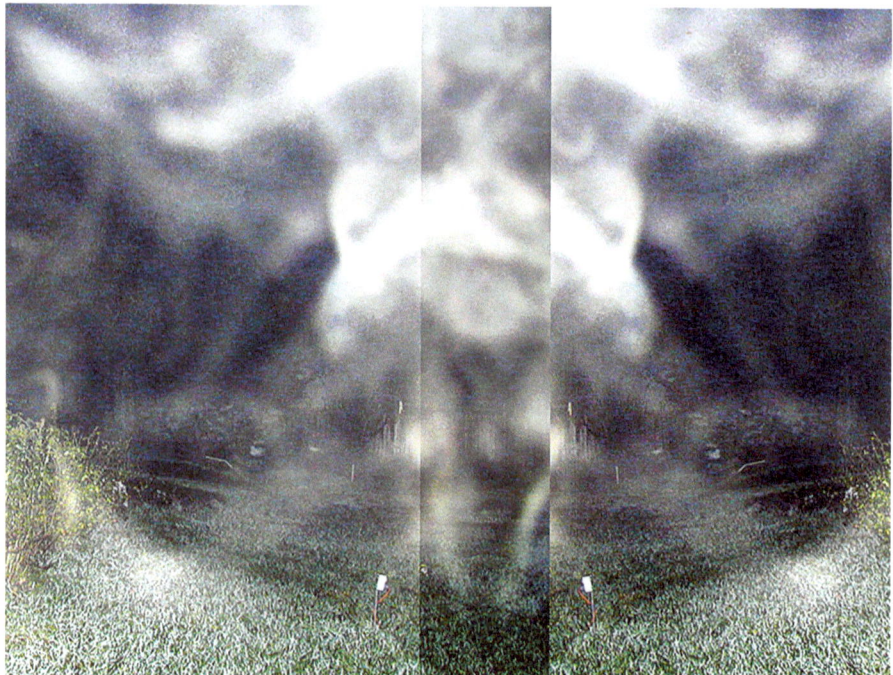

Wyatt (2) – mirrored and measured - side by side

Wyatt is an excellent example of a hands-on approach or a *touch sensitive* method to be applied when developing a Portrait. The goal is to reveal the features of the personality that is hidden within the original apparition photograph. The method requires a light touch and a good computer system.

As stated, I thought it would be helpful and interesting to see how a Portrait can be developed. As an example, I believe the features in this original photograph have been faithfully interpreted to reveal the personality of the underlying entity. To be honest, most of the image is already there. That's my point. Within these images the underlying personality is already there.

When I look at Wyatt, I immediately notice the eye, the brim, the mustache, and the chin …yeah, that's Wyatt. The eye opener is when you measure and mirror the photo, Wyatt is quite the remarkable anomaly, it offers and an incredible display of a supernatural illusion and a highly unusual sense of realism. It's the eyes that get ya.

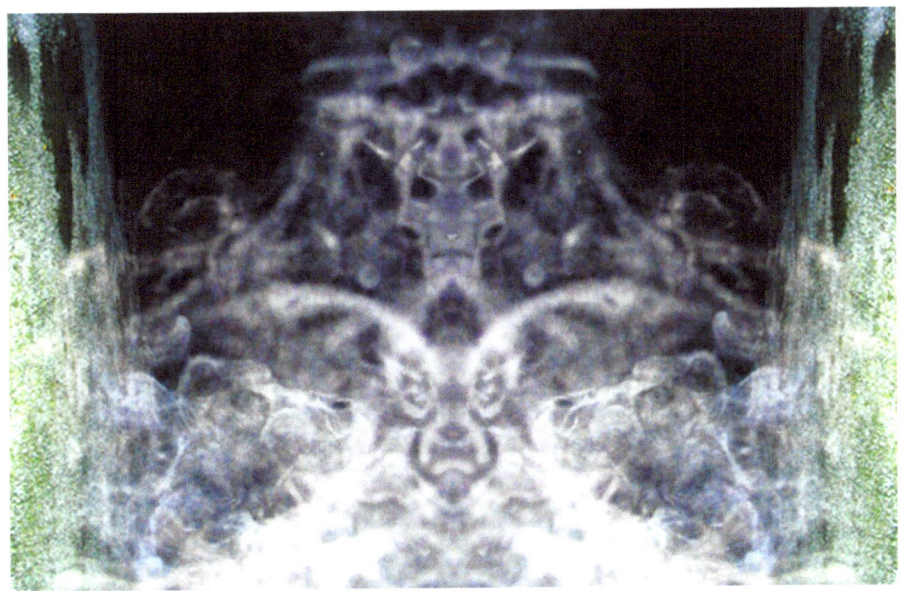

FINGERS

PORTRAIT BY JD

Fingers, is an amazing illusion. It's one of my favorite Portraits. The distinct message posed by Fingers is clearly on display. It's universal, both barrels, in your face. Fck You. That's one reasonable interpretation. I see little to no room for misinterpreting the message. As for being subliminal, you decide. I guess it just needed to be said.

Considering this possibility, it infers knowledge of the language that is bewildering, if not downright and dirty. How is this possible? He's smiling for fks sake. It's a chilling display of monstrous intelligence and an incredible ability to communicate a message, and that message is understood immediately upon reflection, now isn't that interesting? It appears we have a common understanding.

Does Fingers intend to cause harm? Possibly, Fingers is a wise-ass, always was, always will be. But, you have to wonder, if he can message us in this manner does he retain an ability to properly impose an influence upon your senses? If so, is that influence consistent with the reflected image? Once again and clearly stated, proceed with caution.

Fingers (1) - original photo

On first sight, this image looks like a typical anomalous nighttime photograph, and it is. However, there is still more to see, and more to consider. The identification process also includes various rotations to view different perspectives. This image requires a 90° counter-clockwise rotation to notice the personality. The nested figures reveal this one as a complex interpretation, a superior and steadfast intelligence.

If you tilt your head to the right and view the photograph along the top edge, you see a good amount of the illusion. I imagine a definition of supernatural is whatever you make it to be …like seeing spirits.

It should make you wonder what the fk is going on over there. When I started to realize them, I asked that question a lot. I consider Fingers to be a highly evolved supernatural intelligence. Is this the force that imposes a bad attitude and aggressive behavior? Interestingly, this image is quite possibly representative of a negative active force, as they all might be active forces, but this one might be a bad one.

...a thousand words

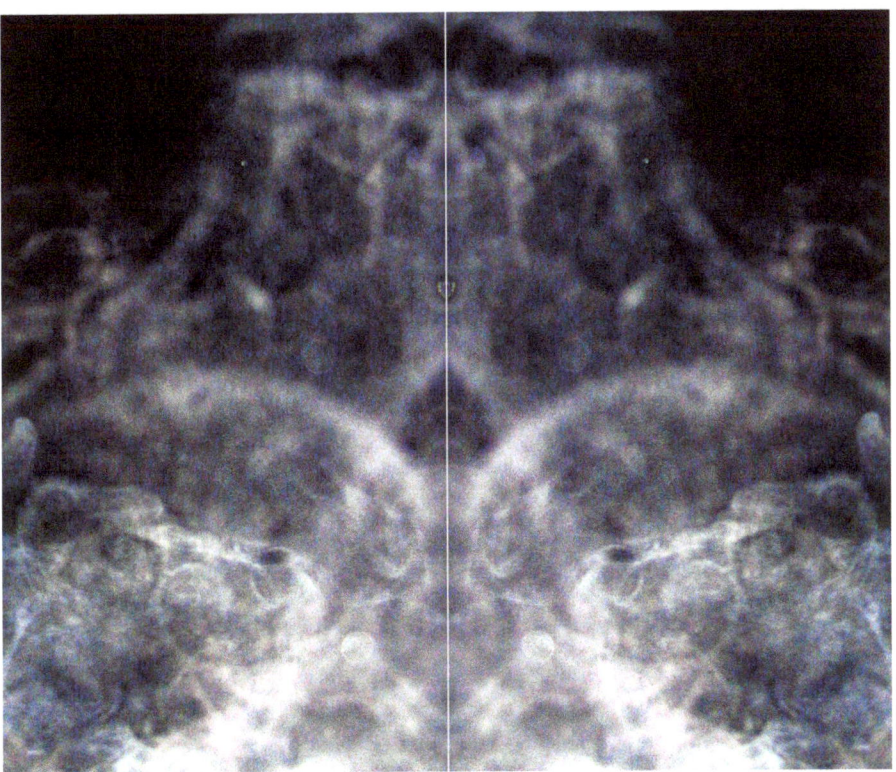

Fingers (2) rotated 90° CCW – mirrored - side by side

Actually, I already captured Fingers. He hangs on my wall with the others. Remember? There is no way for him to get down from there until I take him down. Those are the rules. I own his ass. Just like all of the others I shot. The problem is… I'm releasing him, and the others. I don't know what if anything that can achieve. But I'm willing to find out. Aren't you? Mental exercises, remember? No harm – no foul.

King Dragon

Portrait by JD

King Dragon was among the first to be recognized as an intelligent presence. The message I interpret from the original is, "I'm trying to tell you something, you only have half of the story, use your instinct, skills and ability to complete the picture and see who am I. Do not be afraid, there are more… Welcome"

Well, who am I to refuse an invitation like that? There were more, many more, I learned much from them. They seem to remove the filters that can accompany the human senses of reality. On sight, they expose an alternate intelligent supernatural reality, possibly related to astral or dimension traveling; there are certainly enough categorized roll calls of angels and demons, ghosts and spirits, jinn and genies to fill that void.

In my mind they're all those things and more. However, a human mind can go only so far in establishing an understanding with a supernatural intelligence, the term itself implies a lack of common knowledge.

In the case of this Portrait, the level of development complexity is as basic as possible and yet the entity and the message is unmistakably prophetic and intimidating… "there are more."

I imagine it was intended to begin that way in order for us (people) to see and accept it as a supernatural phenomenon. For instance, what I'd call development complexity includes the final position of the original photograph before I apply the mirrored image revealing the entity.

In the case of Dragon, it's just a mirrored image, a simple flip and side by side placement. The detail, the realism and the illusionary impact is distinct and profoundly supernatural.

It doesn't get any simpler than that. I would consider this to be a supernatural intelligence… a vicious supernatural intelligence.

Some find King Dragon challenging to consider as a benevolent entity. Is it Angelic? Is it Demonic? Or, is it simply a harmless illusion? Perhaps Dragon's appearance as an aggressive spirit is unsettling? But assuming a spirit to be angelic or demonic based on looks is judgy, it might not be his fault he looks like a fkn demon. I've learned to hold judgment in reserve, particularly when you have no reason to assume this is a demon coming to attack you, or an angel coming to protect you. I do agree it looks like one, or the other.

I especially admire the colors of Dragon; he's red, white, and blue. Instinctively, I associate him as an American, a supernatural inhabitant of the land of the free, King Dragon …of America.

Many historical and contemporary cultures claim a reference to Dragons as profound exemplars of supernatural deities …and I agree. King Dragon is an American Dragon. His capture occurred upon American soil, under an American Flag, he's even red, white and blue. It's ironic, he just happens to wear a crown – and that makes him King.

King Dragon is a remarkable illusion. Three solutions (multiple heads) are obvious. The colors, the density levels and the details are stunning and clearly representative of anatomical appendages …violent anatomical appendages. As I said, Portraits are the most interesting phenomenon I have seen in Spirit Research. King Dragon is among the fiercest illusions I hold in captivity. Behold. King Dragon.

Dragon (1) - original photo

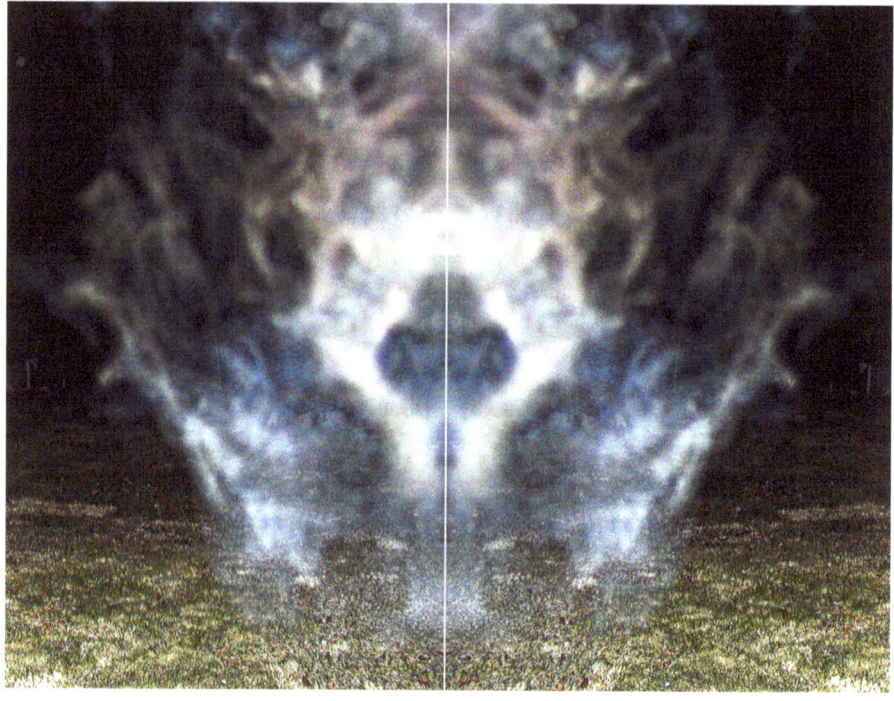

Dragon (2) – mirrored – side by side

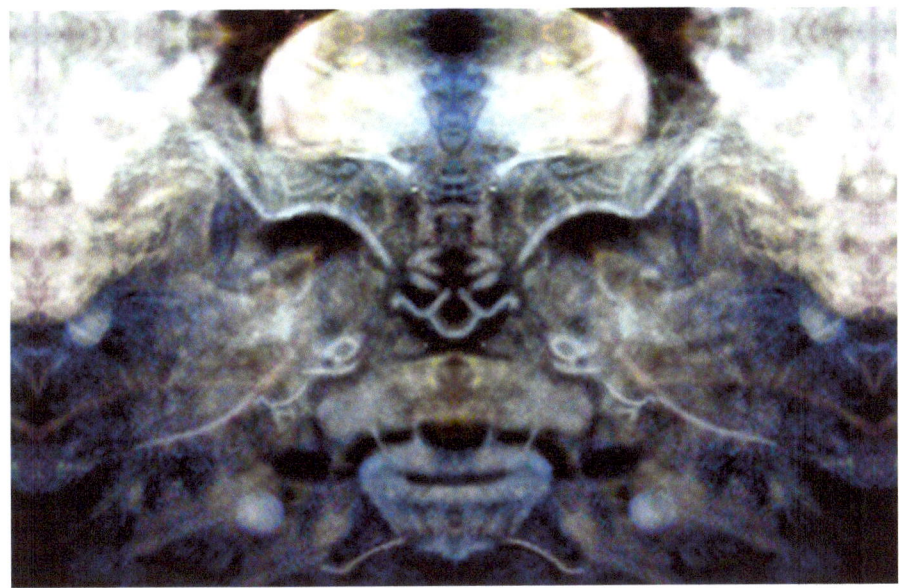

James

Portrait by JD

The Portrait of James is a combination of ectoplasm theory, DNA factors, and unrealized spiritual forces and objectives. In my mind, this Portrait reflects the identity of an ancient supernatural intelligence that possesses the ability to render a psychological influence upon a subject. This is the Portrait of James.

The revelation of this supernatural entity is beyond haunting. I find it difficult or even impossible to reconcile a proper response explaining the Portrait of James. Supernatural, spiritual, paranormal, etc., any of those words fit and none of those words fit. Arguably, nothing like this has ever been seen before …ever. You should wonder why. I do.

The Portrait of James appears to depict a message that is straight to the point; he gets into your mind, his illusionary capabilities can affect both thought and vision. Could this be how he actually looks, or is that what he wants you to think?

The Portrait of James is just cause to reconsider what is possible within a normal range of human awareness, especially when considering the key factors available in developing this Portrait are an anomalous

James (1) - original photo

paranormal photograph and a chance opportunity to see further into that world from the private balcony of one's own backyard. What we find there appears to be the resting place of an unknown ancient entity… the Angel of the Illusions.

I decided upon this image being my namesake for several reasons, one is my inclination to feel a connection. It's a comfort level, a gut feeling; it's contact with a spirit entity and no guilt or fear. In my mind that best describes one thing, an ancestor. The obvious inference is - if indeed ectoplasm theory is a real thing, then the visualized substance should contain traces of the initiates DNA. In other words …ancestor.

Traditional concepts of ectoplasm consider the substance as being expelled from an initiate's body. Tradition also allows for random spirits to be imposed upon an initiate and used as a conduit. However, any concept of ectoplasm is not supported by any discerning scientific body primarily due to the lack of qualified and /or corroborative evidence. James disagrees. This is the Portrait of James.

Djra-Kul-A-Din

Portrait by JD

There are spirits dwelling in the trees, I have seen several of them in support of this opinion. My impression is they are "the old ones." They watch in silence from above. But that's not all, they record the events they witness within their rings. This is not unreasonable, it's well documented that tree rings indicate the age, seasonal patterns, and various environmental situations and events at a given time in history. It would not be surprising to learn they also record the impressions of human activity as well. Nature's evidence locker, indeed. These impressions may be used in the testimony of one's past deeds, both good and bad. If and when a post life reckoning is required, one's past may be accurately retrieved from this natural mechanism of facts and occurrences.

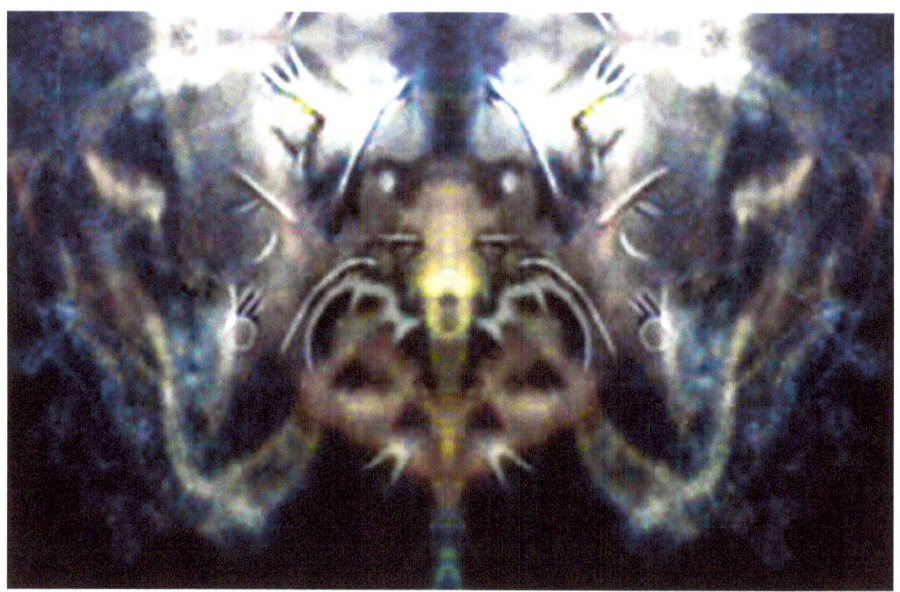

Chief

Portrait by JD

It all points to symbolism. The markings are obvious, however, there is an identity clause that symbolizes the impression of one's interior soul. The markings that appear in a halo like fashion framed around the face require an interpretation from the observer in order to proceed.

In this case, difficulties arise when trying to determine the origin as being a static or dynamic initiative. A static interpretation might qualify this set of symbols as a unique identifier or presence, to us, it's a name, whereas a dynamic approach might indicate a more complex communication system is involved. As I said, "It's difficult to understand when you don't speak the language."

Strong indications for both concepts are reasonable, which now infers dynamics are indeed observable and a valid form of contact. Ectoplasm theory of emanations including DNA factors, support the dynamic point of view that ancestral linkage is a natural occurrence with a distinct identity.

...a thousand words

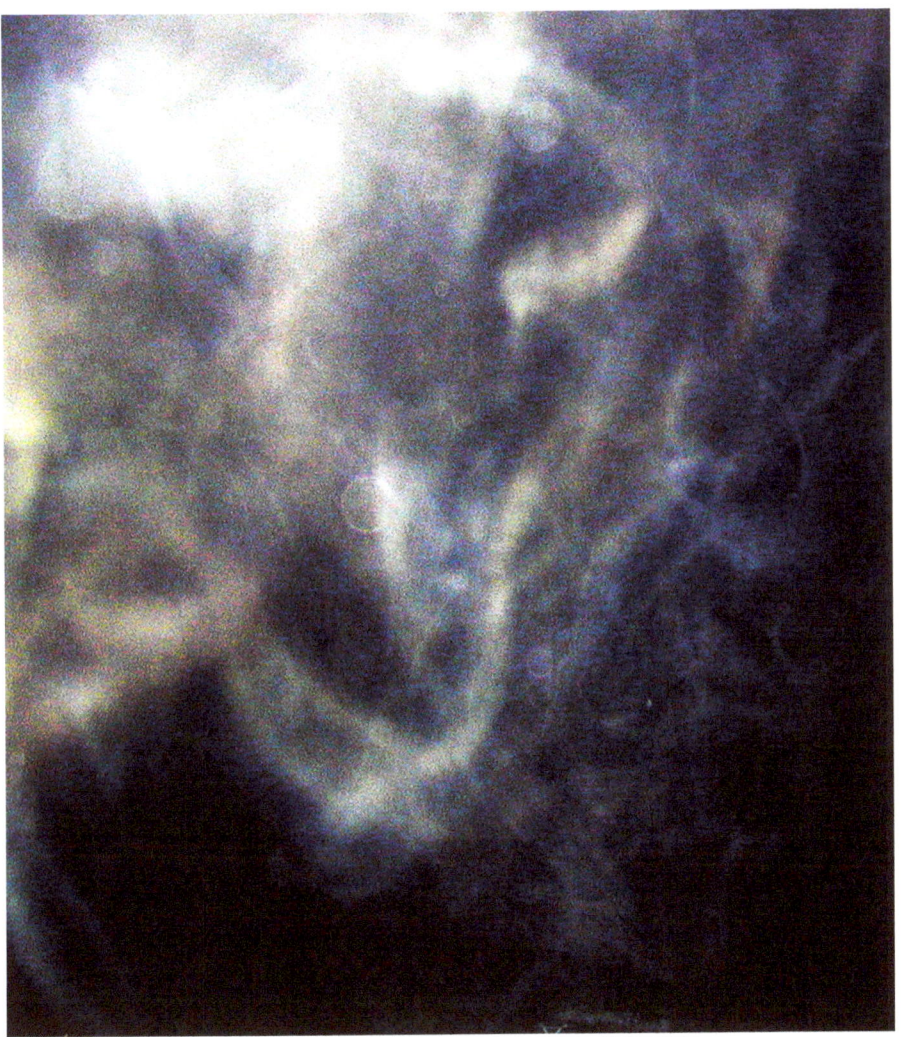

Chief (1) - original photo

Endora

Portrait by JD

I've stressed the effort necessary in developing an accurate Portrait, but naming a Portrait is no easy task. There are no rules, there is no precedent. Instinct, logic, and reason often dominate my struggle to put names to the faces… such as they are. In many of the cases, instinct wins. In all of the cases, it's irrelevant primarily due to names being a human mechanism of identification. These are not humans.

At times, the naming convention I employ appears obvious, the name or identity of the image seemingly fits the personality, other times it's personal and it feels like a test. Mostly, but not always I pass the test and the name fits. It doesn't matter to them, it matters to me. …it is what it is.

...a thousand words

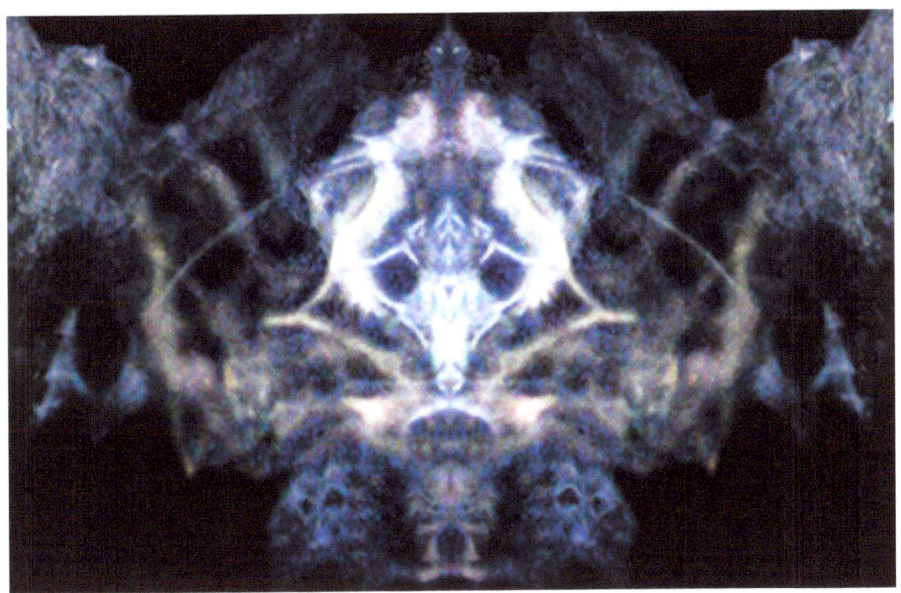

Fang

PORTRAIT BY JD

This is a supernatural bat; wings are obvious, as are teeth. Why would an entity made of vapor need teeth? Several Portraits display teeth, pointed teeth. Biologics that have teeth have them for a reason. In this case, I hardly think the rules of physical anatomy apply in a similar manner. Sometimes, we're left with more questions than answers.

A prominent display of teeth is achieved for many reasons; teeth can be a predatory display of aggression such as, the intent to kill you, devour you, or dominate you. The entity in this image appears capable of accomplishing all three of those tasks. Notice the figure wearing the black hood at the top of Fang's crown, it appears he is the driving force directing Fang's activities.

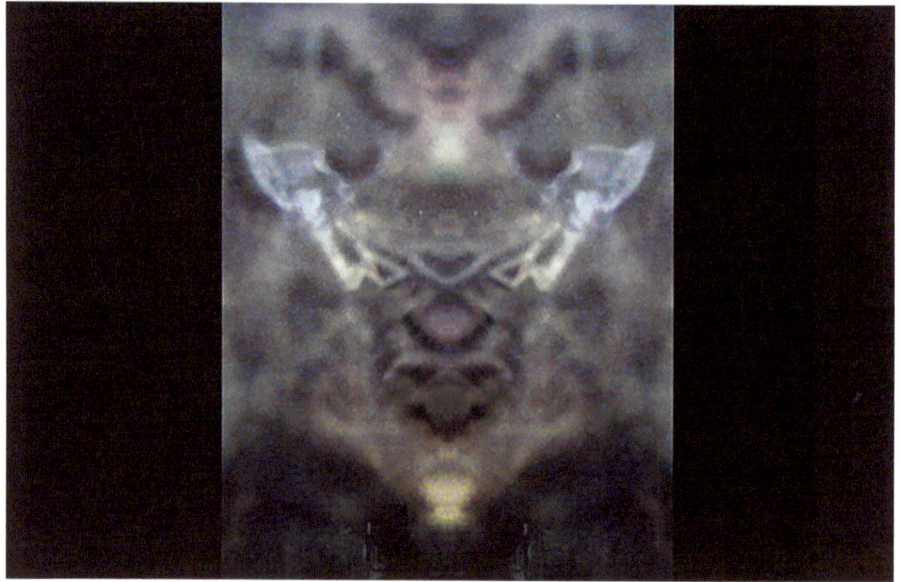

BEAST OF THE ANGELS

PORTRAIT BY JD

I imagine this Portrait as being a face of the supernatural monster. It appears to portray consistencies that are both angelic and demonic. A Fallen Angel perhaps? Those indications are quite strong, and deserve consideration no doubt. But notice what appear to be open gates behind the Beast; one might infer it's the entrance to captivity, the gates from which he has escaped, or the gates that he guards.

This Portrait indicates primal supernatural authority, psychological dominance, and/or pure violence, qualities found to be inherently shared among the most brutal of warriors, deranged murderers, or evil spirits. Qualities found inherent to the Devil. I've had difficulties dismissing this concept.

This Illusion is the phenomenal revelation of a supernatural deity. Though one of many, it imposes a dark influence upon the observer. The headpiece is adorned with angelic style wings similar to a style and structure found to exist on other Portraits. Sitting on top appears to be a smaller anomalous deity of favor or regret.

...a thousand words

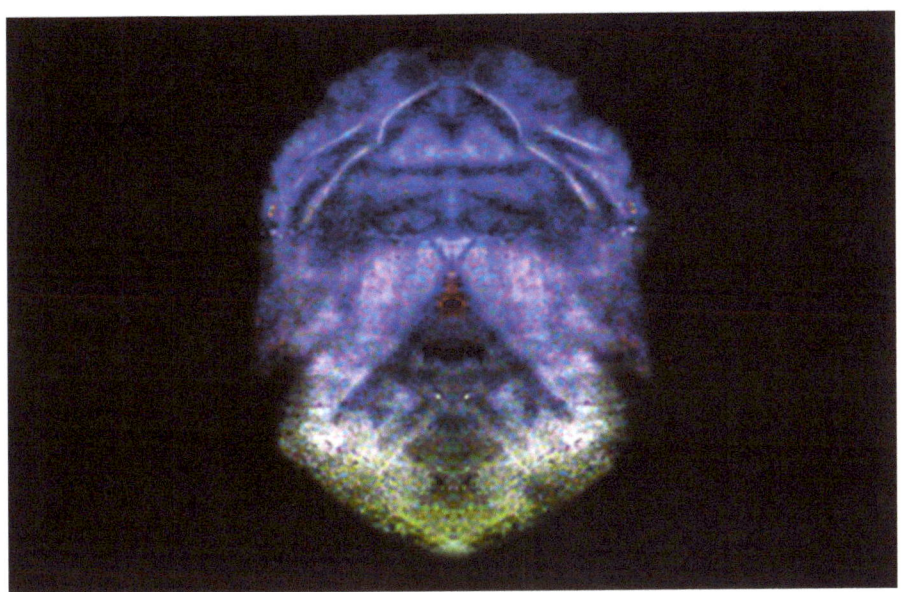

INSTANT KARMA

PORTRAIT BY JD

Sitting back in my seat, high above the street
rising up to meet …the Sun
Slippin into gear, passing all the years
my ride through the spheres …has begun
I'm flyin' high, again, on the Wings of the Wind
Another place and time, that I know is mine
Creeps up on me, to be …the one
The piper was paid, the bloods on the blade
Now, I'm on my way …back home
I'm flyin' high, again, on the Wings of the Wind
I'm flyin' high - I'm on the - Wings - of the - Wind
I'm flyin' high – its time - to make - my move - again

...a thousand words

LORD OF THE SEVEN DAYS

PORTRAIT BY JD

This Portrait appears to wear a crown of Angelic proportions. The image reveals the anomaly of a hidden persona recovered from *Figure LSD (1)*: "a discreet capture." Notice the detail of the "wings." Yes, I said wings. Not much is known about wings since there is no proof of their true existence. However, this Portrait and several others appear to support an argument that favors the existence of "wings."

These are not the typical set of wings we have traditionally come to recognize, these wings are spectacular. Seeing the real thing is an eye opening experience, as I said, "a photograph changes everything." Remember the old saying "truth is stranger than fiction." Wings as I see them, display a unique and dynamic structure of supernatural realism.

My impression here is one of authority, a majestic authority. This image displays a vision of wings, crowns, and angelic structure, never before seen but through the lens of a camera.

A conceptual examination of wings throughout this body of work is highly encouraged, it's revealing and informative. Wings shown on most Portraits often appear to be bright white; e.g., T-bone, Seven

LSD (1) - original photo - a discreet capture

Days, although other Portraits display wings that are conspicuously obvious they're not as brightly energized such as Wings of the Wind.

Any way you slice it wings, are a very interesting piece of the pie. But not all Portraits have wings, and that presents an interesting unavoidable point, what are they really used for? Could it be a status symbol within the hierarchical status of spirits, or possibly an identification property of a specific ancestral group?

Looking at this image one should find it difficult to imagine it's based on an apparition appearing for about one second unless it was already formed. It's not difficult to imagine this illusion occupying a dynamic, alternate state of reality. The complexity of detail and the engaging facial expression affirms a presence of an intelligent supernatural entity.

Sparx

Portrait by JD

The Angel of Sparx, appears to me to be a motorcycle with a rider coming straight at me. I even see the front wheel. The collar reminds me of Evel. I remember when I first saw that, and thinking it was cool. I agreed to it immediately. Who wouldn't?

Motorcycles are a part of American history, and so is Evel. And for the same reason, a Harley.

I don't ride but I've known brothers who do, and getting wiped out on the road either sucs, or it's the glorious path to other side. In this case, Sparx appears to have a big shit eatin' grin on his face, so I'm going with …a glorious path to the other side. Cheers, bro.

Wings of the Wind
Portrait by JD

A supernatural enigma of Angelics is captured in this Portrait. The upper host is reminiscent of an ancient deity; he wears a crown, a helmet, or both, further indication he is an ancient and powerful spirit.

The lower host appears to be the first visual recording of Cherubim, The Winged Angels of God. The Illusion is captivating and frightening.

It's fkn incredible.

...a thousand words

Wings (1) - original photo

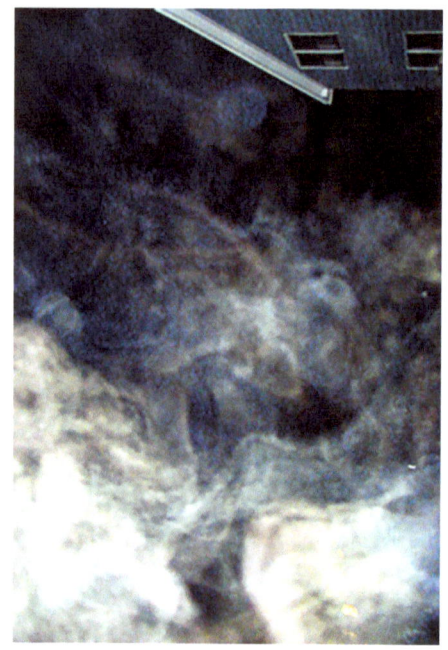

Wings (2)

Wings (3)

John the Elder
Portrait by JD

I said, at times, I'd offer an explanation when no explanation is available... this is not one of those times.

This image is one of the most thought provoking illusions in my collection. It indicates a multi-force phenomenon of anomalous supernatural entities working together as a group. Trying to count the figures in this image is an interesting exercise towards first seeing the illusions, and then wondering how or why they did it.

I offer no explanation, sometimes it happens that way. As I've said, I too am a fan of supernatural phenomena, and I've not seen anything like this. I think most would agree, and I would not be here otherwise.

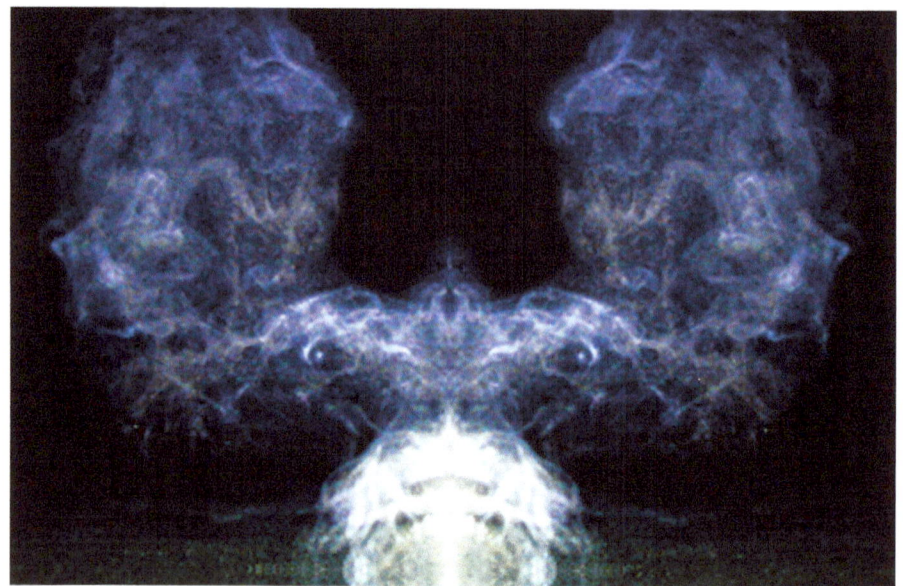

Hammerhead

Portrait by JD

They too appear to be cunning, or at least appear to be. Some want to be friendly and attempt to communicate. And there are others who are more traditional, more set in their way, to them interaction between the humans and the spirits is a secret, and they want to keep it that way.

I needed to draw them out into the open, where I could capture them and study them. That's when I began to develop skills in trapping. I could catch them now that I could perceive them. So, I practiced perception in the off season, and I waited for the spring.

…this is Hammer, he's a good boy.

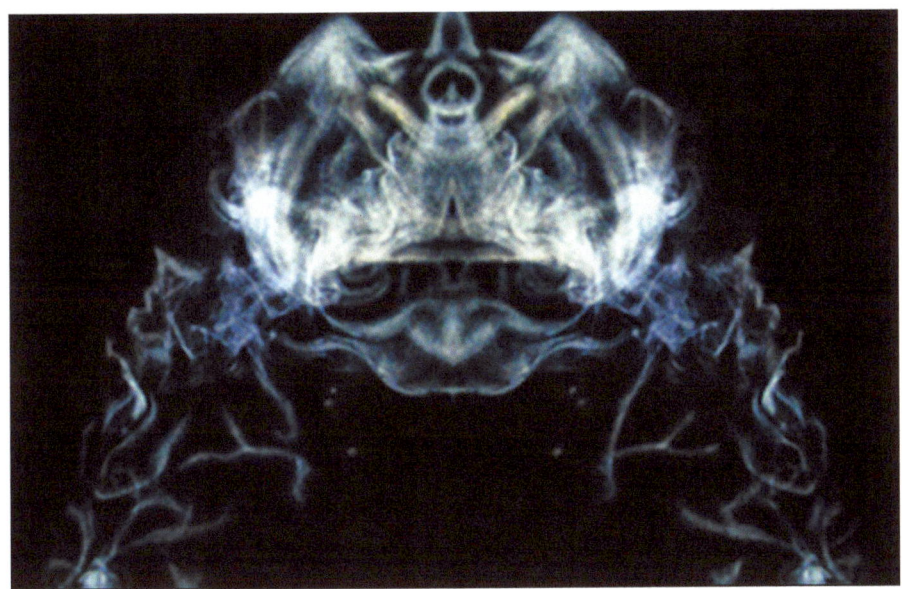

Flag

Portrait by JD

    I remember the night I figured it out for the first time, I barely felt a thing; it was the smell and taste I remember most, it was warm and bloody, with a natural crude odor that stung at my lip; it was both sweet and sticky like cheap candy. It's nature's way of hiding things right under your nose. I was scenting …like an animal. If it makes a difference to you, be glad you're not the one. Consider that an apology.

    It's been decades after the fact, and I've become ruthless and cunning as I practiced a modern method of an old technique …spirit hunting. I began in cemeteries and graveyards, it seemed a natural place to begin, the scent is heavy in a graveyard.

CHILLIPOP

Portrait by JD

I left things for them as gifts. I would hide things in the yard. I started placing them on the ground at the cemetery too. At first it seemed unrealistic they would respond, even though I had the distinct feeling I was being watched as I placed the items in hiding spots hoping to avoid simple detection. On several occasions the anomalies appeared shortly after placing the gifts. It was then I knew I could trap them using the gifts as bait. And that's when the real shootin' started. At first, it's like trying to catch a bird in your hands with your eyes closed. It can be done if you wait long enough, until they're comfortable …so I waited.

THE DRIP

Portrait by JD

    I have an incurable cancer. Allegedly, from my time serving as a US Marine stationed at Camp Lejeune. No hard feelings. Semper Fi.

    The Drip is the magic formula helping keep me and others like me, alive …a little longer. I'm grateful. Chemo treatments can be rough, but you keep going, surrender is not an option. You hang in there …until the string runs out and there are no options …that's how I choose to look at it.

    Saying that I'm lucky my cancer was caught early is awkward for me, I don't really feel lucky here. But I am. Thanks to regular heart checkups and Adam. He initiated the cadence ultimately leading to oncology, and my new reality …Cancer.

    I've been diagnosed for several years now, and have dedicated a considerable amount of time imagining the possibilities. Currently, the cancer I suffer from is being controlled …shout out to Smilow.

    It doesn't mean this cancer will ultimately kill me, but I do suffer the side effects of weakness, fatigue and fear of reality. I can live with that …a little longer. I'm grateful. Another shout out to Smilow.

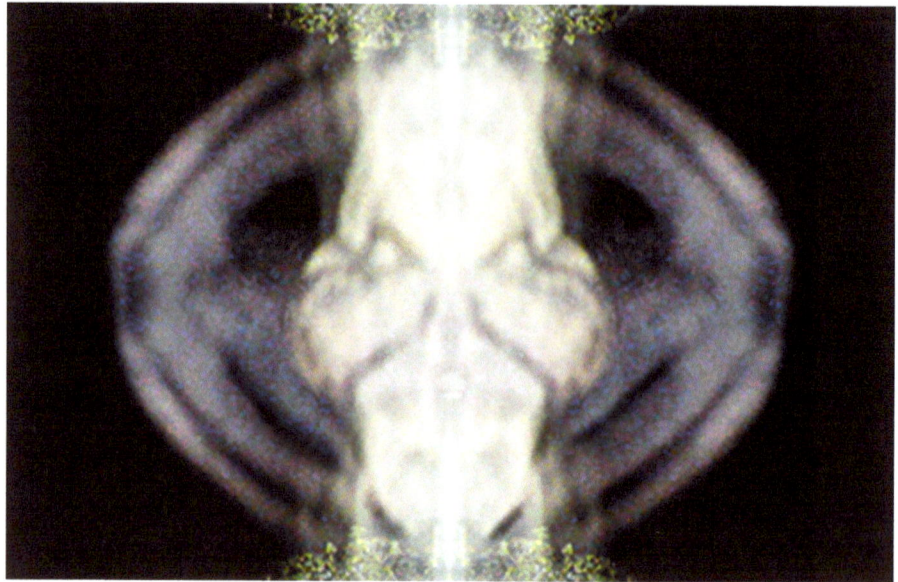

Aquadio

Portrait by JD

Many people believe they have a guardian angel or spirit protector looking after their well being. It's a calming and comforting feeling to imagine a supernatural being is watching you and can influence the world you live in, which is probably why many of us tend to think it. Spirit guides, Angels, or muses, some are watching us, and some are watching over us, who decides?

It has been several years since I shot my first spirit apparition photo. During that time I have spent countless hours seeking to reproduce the elusive formula that induces apparitions to appear. I realized it's a secret, so I found another way …and I waited.

SPIRIT OF THE SECOND SIGHT

PORTRAIT BY JD

The diviner, the conjurer, or the seer of the dark dimensions, this illusion is the Portrait of a telepathic master. It's a revealing and unique portrayal of the nested host concept, showing the primary and nested deities stacked on top of each other, totem style.

The nested deities appear to possess at least three obvious sets of eyes; ironically, the eyes of the primary host are not to be found. The concentration is obvious, and appears to be a factor in negotiating the nested formations. There is no direct evidence supporting the existence of alternate or higher dimensions, however, inferences drawn from anomalous exhibits show otherwise. Check out that 'stache.

Dr. Seven

Portrait by JD

Often, there is no calculating the weirdness a Portrait might reflect. When searching for the potential hidden anomaly, the resulting figure can dismay and confuse the observer. Eventually, you come to realize the anomaly is not a predetermined atypical occurrence, but a dynamic effect of supernatural consciousness.

There are obvious observances I look for in an image such as, eyes, mouths, or skulls. They don't have to be exact representations of those features, that wouldn't be fair, but recognition and placement of parallel features is fair. For example, the eyes on this image appear in a location I would recognize as a facial feature. Complimentary features are also present including a nested face and the skull, very strange.

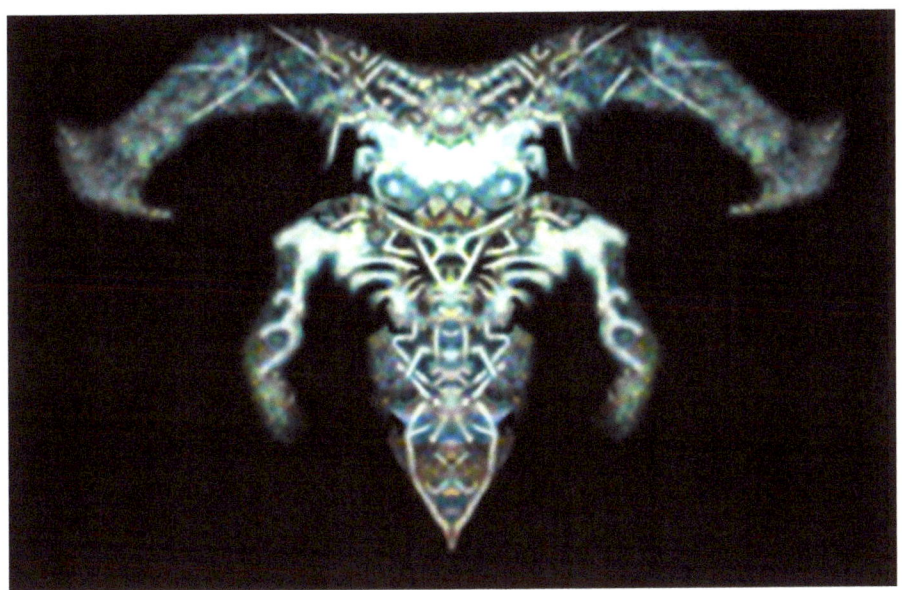

Ace

Portrait by JD

Late one night I was greeted with a deafening roar emanating from directly above my head, as I looked up I could still hear it howling, but nothing was there. It circled me from above and I waited for the attack as this is surely a large canine I'm hearing, but the attack never came. I realized if the sound were to be emanating from a hostile predator I would not have heard it before the attack. So I waited...

I have no doubt the sound from above was meant for my ears. It was to inform me that I am being watched, from above. The sound of the howling wolf is also a message, to beware. My response is to heed the warning, and continue on, I'm getting close.

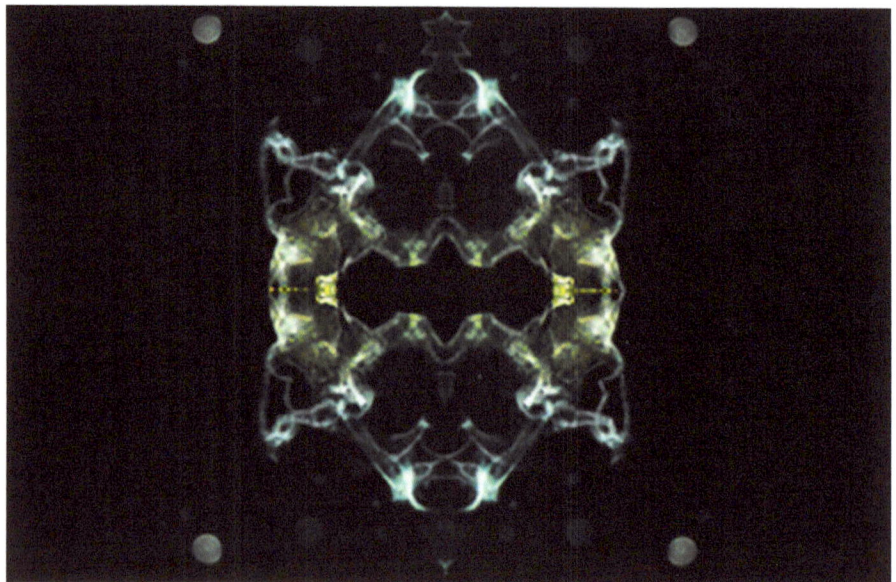

Karats

Portrait by JD

This is a mask, a golden mask. There are openings for the eyes and the mouth in locations we easily identify. The colors and engravings are spectacular. The gradations are due to the photographic quality of the capture. Cameras have changed the way we can view anomalous phenomena. They offer a momentary glimpse of unexplainable events and occurrences.

This image is a visually effective illusion and one can almost imagine the face looking at you from behind the mask. On the other hand, one can also imagine putting the mask on and looking out.

As masks are concerned, this one is unique to me. I don't recall ever having seen this design before, and especially not in gold.

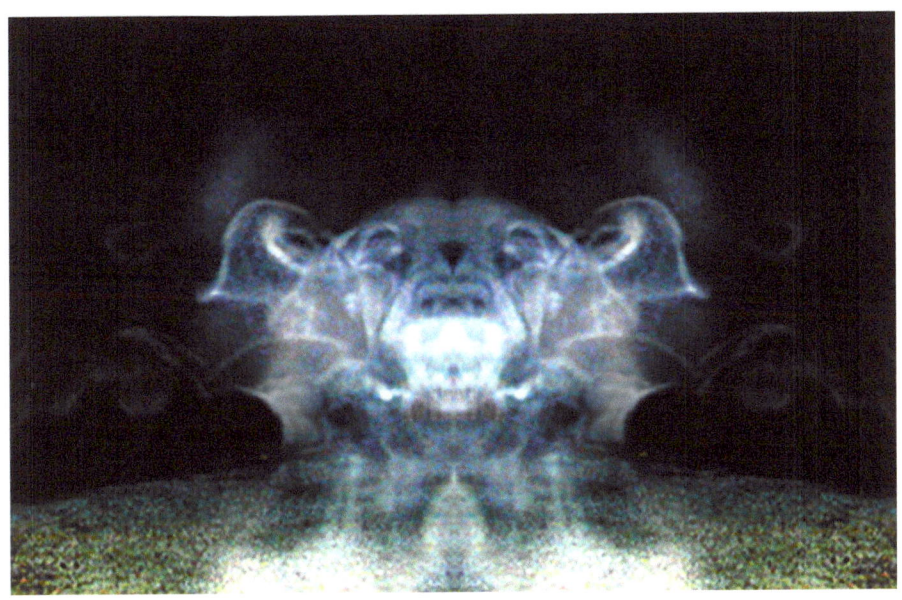

Prince Dragon
Portrait by JD

Witnessing the materialization process can be quite intense. I think the best way to describe what we're seeing is materialized spirit matter, or, "statically charged liquid smoke." The darkness provides a excellent background when I light 'em up …sorry, when I capture them.

It's nearly impossible to predict how a paranormal experience is going to unfold. Sometimes weird shit happens. But, that's how you know it's starting to work. Picture taking, is but a single part of the process. To me, it means the process works …sometimes.

I imagine part of the reasoning for achieving a positive outcome is that I chose to actively participate in the experiments. I also enjoy hunting.

…a thousand words

Bones

Portrait by JD

Bones is a favorite of mine. He's different than the others. It appears primal and yet it's symbolically articulate. I saved this Portrait for last for several reasons, uniqueness being the key. There's a lot going on in that small space. I count four solutions straight up the middle on this one.

It's a tough call to make on a photograph but I think this one is a spinner. A "spinner" is an anomalous object that looks the same regardless of the direction you view it from. I prefer a clockwise solution, so if you rotate Bones to the right, gradually increasing the speed of revolutions until this image appears exactly as is, then, yeah, I think it would look the same from every angle …invisible.

...a thousand words

Bones (1) - original photo

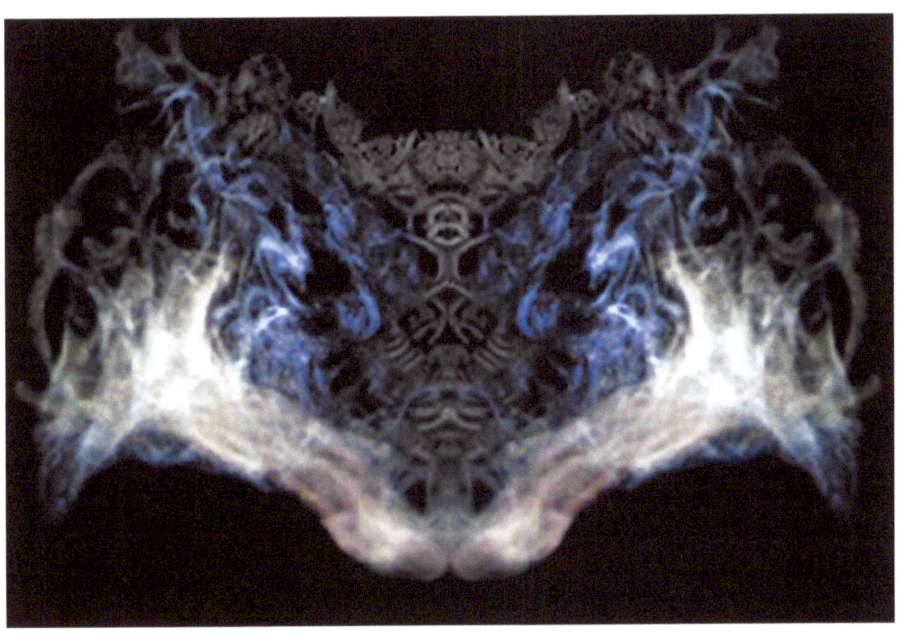

Bones (1) - flipped and mirrored

*"The trick is to sleep standing up with your eyes open,
if they think you're sleeping, they come closer."*

Portraits 4.1

Diary of a Madman

Diary of a Madman

Now you've seen what I've seen

I'm aware some of my descriptions are direct. However, in my defense, I am innocent. I wonder if you saw things from my perspective, wouldn't you agree? I realize much of what I've presented here can be difficult to digest. Then again, disregarding obvious facts can also be difficult to digest.

The anomalous apparitions I photographed are a fact. I do not offer an explanation other than they are a recurring abstract illusionary phenomenon. What are they exactly is for you to determine. Find your own truth, and I'll find mine, that's fair.

One must assume we are in dangerous territory and should proceed with caution. What I consider a rare unconfirmed event is contact with a supernatural entity. In that moment one has to be ready for either a benevolent experience or a malevolent encounter.

That's my opinion, I was there, and I saw it happen. Better still, I took photographs, so you could see it too, and though I may be misguided, I am not being deceitful. That's the purpose behind the photographs, you don't have to take my word for anything. You may use a sense of cynicism and reject this as BS. Or utilize a sense of logic and imagination for optimal consideration of facts.

If in fact the event did occur as in the case of a physical apparition, how do you know what caused it to occur and why would you assume it ended? The physical event may last but a moment, but, is that the end of the occurrence? That's a good question. When does the occurrence begin and when does it end?

It's quite possible the intent behind the occurrence would be subtle, but consistent, thus perpetuating the concept of a discreet subliminal influence, no questions asked. I also consider these influences to be dynamic. It's not a one-way, one-time effect. I've been working with the images for over two decades and they still seem to be effective. I also realize this is a thin line. They are, in my opinion mental exercises. There are going to be thin lines.

I believe there are enough recorded instances to qualify this as an attack. Yes, an attack. Multiple occurrences over a sustained period of time, that's the definition of an attack. But, are we calling it that? No way. I have never felt like I was under attack. In fact, the opposite is true. I thought most, if not all instances were friendly… most of the time.

I'll admit I have considered many circumstances by which this could have happened, and I am at a loss for suggestions. I like to think part of my effort was to establish a credible portrayal of American super-nature. In fact, it does seem to indicate a race of semi-invisible inhabitants, normally unseen, was consistently appearing in a neutral zone of reality …my backyard.

This circumstance does require a physical and psychological definition of the "zone", or at least its proper boundaries. First, it's the physical definition of the USA and all territories and boundaries within.

This works for me and for several reasons, not the least of which is the right to perform these experiments under the eyes and conditions of the US Constitution regardless of religious obligations. Second, I was fkn born here. It's my home.

These options seem necessary when considering the stakes at hand, specifically, one's religious convictions and responsibilities, or guilt free intellectual advancements and opportunities that neglect those specific convictions. To be clear, it has nothing to do with written laws, written rules or prohibitions. It has everything to do with being Catholic.

As a general rule, performing an exercise that includes contact with supernatural beings is frowned upon by the Catholic Church, and I might add, with good reason.

The US Constitution does not support such restrictive behavior. However, I should note, the US Constitution does maintain a moral structure similar in effect to long held Judeo-Christian values, with the additional opportunity for citizens to legally engage in acts that would be condemned outside its borders. As said, I was born here.

As an American, I felt obligated to continue my work exploring the mystery of ghosts and spirits, and in doing so, continue using the US Constitution to justify my actions. I should add this obligation was firmly based on the belief these apparitions are real spirit occurrences. There was no choice, no option, it was my responsibility to get it right.

I'll admit the religious repercussions scare me. The Catholic Church can be unmovable, relentless and in some cases, unforgiving. I'll admit to not being a prime example of a good Catholic, but for me, it's similar to not picking your own parents, you're born into that situation. They will always be my parents and I will always have been born Catholic in the state of New York.

What that means to me is considerable. Catholicism is the epitome of what a supernatural religion should be, hopefully that's an objective opinion. As a lifelong member, I'm proud of that fact. To me, active participation in this type of exercise could be a profound expectation.

Moving forward I had a clear conscience and a firm objective. If in fact my experiments reveal an anomalous phenomenon subjective to ghost theory, am I to refrain from continuing these experiments due to religious beliefs, or do I continue under the mechanism of American freedom from/of religion? It may appear to some this is an easy decision, it's not.

I've considered that in fifty or even a hundred years from now, will anyone care that at times my stated intentions were to hunt and trap souls? Maybe. I personally find that statement offensive, then again, it's not about feelings, it's about facts, and about results …those are what I'd care about.

However, what if I actually did capture them? Does the end justify the means? Does intent matter? I would say "yes, of course it matters." Truth be told I believed it then and I believe it now, they can read your fkn mind. That's a scary thought, because I also believe they can put thoughts in your head just as easily as reading them. How do I know that? Well, that is my opinion, as I said "I don't know if I'm always right, but I try to be." Spiritual forces can be mysterious, if indeed one travels that path, expect the unexpected.

* * *

"I consider myself, an explorer, within the territory, of the United States of America. It's how I justify, to my Faith, that I am free to explore the mystery, the history, of us all. Amen."

* * *

This may be one of those times when additional context is helpful, relevant, and interesting. The following sub-chapters contain information on past events and occurrences. Some instances have been documented and previously published.

The Creeps

Many years ago, I played lead guitar in a local rock band, we called ourselves James Walker and the Creeps. I was James, and Walker is my bud from school, Donny Walker. The Creeps was not intended to be the other band members, it was the mood we intended to achieve as musicians. We wrote some clever songs about the afterlife, we used titles such as, Moving On, The Other Side, The End, Other States, etc. etc.

It seemed we not only shared an admiration for the Beatles and Hendrix, we also had an inclination towards the spirit world and the supernatural. Back then, I had a small collection of books covering topics such as ghosts, spirits and other related phenomena. When Donny and I decided to form a band, he told me he too had a strong inclination towards the spirit world.

Donny told me he participates in séance type sessions in which his uncle goes into a trance and makes contact with various spirit entities. Then he told me, he shares a house with his uncle and we should go there and hang out with our guitars. He said he would get me to sit in on the sessions, which he did. I saw a gifted medium. His uncle was doing some next level stuff.

For a time, these activities were included as part of the backdrop of our natural environment. We wrote songs about the afterlife, we played songs about the afterlife and then we participated in some next level contact with the spirit world… with and without his uncle. Communicative abilities have long been thought to share genetic links. I've always believed that to be true. I believe it to be true with Donny.

Ultimately, we moved in all of our band equipment, amps, drums, guitars, and we even set up a recording platform at his place. We learned a lot, we wrote songs and we practiced. Usually, we could only play when Donny's uncle wasn't at home, he was a little older than us and was not a fan of rock bands. So during the day we fired up the amps, and after 4:00 pm we worked on writing and recording songs using headphones.

The band played small clubs and events, our set was mostly rock covers but we always threw in one or two of our own songs. We managed to be selected to participate in a promotional album of select bands from Long Island. We opened and closed the album; we played the first song on the first side and the last song on the second side. I imagine it got some airplay, somewhere.

Donny and I often discussed The Beatles. The similarities, such as they were, and how they related to our rock and roll fantasy. We thought we could do the same thing. We couldn't. Although, when we were in the studio recording songs, we could play all the instruments, he was the lead singer, I never adapted to singing, it just makes me uncomfortable. I played guitar.

Donny's still in the music business, he's played on multiple records and hit #64 on the Billboard Charts. He lives in Nashville now and produces a country music radio show that is frequently nominated for the annual ACM Awards. No more Telecaster, but still gettin' it done in the music biz.

We've been friends for fifty years. We stay in touch and always discuss family matters and personal situations. We're even Godfather to each other's daughter. Our children refer to each of us respectively as uncle. The discussions Donny and I focus on to this day remain constant, creative and often creepy... Often, we circle around to John.

New Year's Day, 1981, I'd been invited to Donny's house for dinner. A few people were going to be there, including one of his brothers. His uncle was cooking, family dinner attire. Afterwards, it was suggested to do a session for the New Year. Five of us gathered quietly downstairs in the reading room. The session began with a prayer. Then we received this message:

"Happy New Year I gave what I could to many kids, I meant to give more. Tell Yoko sell that house... flood... I live on, John was my name. I sang with some great guys, we were four. Tell Paul I love him from the day we met... but I love Yoko too. I did not want the band to split up. ...Vigil, thank you, Yoko. I started on three, now on four..."

Donny and I were ecstatic. We thought it might have been us that got him there, it's basically what we were trying to do at the time. We thought it would come out in the music, we didn't think we'd get a visit.

We did another session on January 4th, (my dad's birthday) and then once again, on January 9th when we received this message:

"Hi Guys, I hear your music. PA low, turn up till maximum. Two songs you are doing are going better. Try the first verse in C. On the third song, count till finish. The fourth song in Db, lower your voice. "

Imagine how we felt now. We didn't just get a visit, we're getting instructions ...from John.

Donny and I realize the circumstance of John to be special and often consider all parties may have played a distinct part in the presence of John at that location. But clearly, if the guy is commenting on our set list, he sees the need to intervene in our music. The question is: when did that begin? And, when did it end? Was Donny's uncle the confirmation, and us the catalyst? In the scheme of things, does it really matter?

Well, to be honest, of course it matters… I say it was us. We worked together tirelessly trying to develop that third personality… the unseen force that takes over your hands when you play. Many guitar players think that way. We did. Did it work? It sure looks like it did…

We honestly don't know who was responsible for being the catalyst. For Donny and me, even though several decades have since passed, it was enough. We continue to maintain an opinion of confidence and inspiration that lies buried in the accomplishments of the past. Yeah, yeah, yeah, it was us, maybe.

You have to admit, it's a good story. I have a recording of the entire radio broadcast of the interview Donny's uncle gave on WBAB radio in West Babylon, NY in early 1981, and identifying the James Walker Band as the musical group named in the John Lennon sessions. The previous quotations are transcribed from the direct broadcast interview hosted by author and media personality Joel Martin. The transcriptions are accurate and the story is true. I should know. I was there when it happened.

BTW, Donny's uncle is George Anderson, and as stated on his social media, he is the world's most scientifically tested medium. His first book: "we don't die" is an excellent insight of a psychic medium.

…and what about the influence the sessions had on us? …that's a story for another day …maybe.

Theater of the Mind

I visited Raymond Moody's Theater of the Mind Research Center in Alabama. I had the best time. I stayed with Dr. Moody and his family for several days of real southern hospitality. It was my pleasure to return the favor several years later in Connecticut.

The great thing about speaking with Raymond is he's extremely well versed in so many topics it's difficult to keep up. You need to remember underneath that friendly and humble exterior is the mind of a disarming genius; he's a philosopher, a psychiatrist, and an academic scholar.

We talked about ghosts and spirits, near death experiences, Greek mythology, the ancient Oracle, and anything supernatural. Eventually, we got around to discussing the Psychomanteum.

I was looking forward to visiting Raymond's Psychomanteum chamber, which is actually named the "Dr. John Dee Memorial Theater of the Mind." At first, the room, which is on the third floor of the Center, was disorienting. You sit in a nice comfortable chair with no legs, and gaze into an elevated mirror in order to experience optimum depth.

I remember Raymond telling me to relax and wait for it to happen. Eventually, you begin to drift into a semi-conscious state of observance. Then the mirror takes over. Many people report seeing distinct shadows, as did I. However, as I watched the shadow gradually darken within the mirror, it flew out of the mirror and flew straight at my head. I threw my head to the right and looked over my left shoulder… "holy shit. Where did it go? That was cool."

I got up and left the room to find Raymond, who was sitting in an easy chair with a smile on his face, he said, what'd you see?

I told him what happened …he called him the swooper. We were laughing about it. Raymond knew very well about my experiences photographing spirit anomalies, I think he was expecting me to see something strange.

Sometime later, Raymond had a speaking engagement at a campus in New York, we made arrangements for him to stay with my family in Connecticut for a few days. We picked up right where we left off, discussing the supernatural. This time, it was Raymond who was visiting my Psychomanteum …my backyard.

I had long since stopped taking photographs and Raymond knew that. We discussed my photographs many times, but I was still very happy he got to see where it happened. I also developed an ass-kickin' multimedia presentation that was ready and waiting for him. I knew Raymond would appreciate the effort as well as the spirit photography.

We had some interesting discussions and I sometimes wondered if he was shrinkin' me, he is after all a psychiatrist. It's been years since those days at Dr. Moody's Theater of the Mind and back here in Connecticut …I remember them fondly, always will.

Psychic Eye Radio

Jeffrey Wands and I became friends in the 90's. He hosted a radio call-in show on Long Island, a psychic call-in show called Psychic Eye. He is an excellent telepathic psychic medium. I've watched him perform some impressively accurate personal readings. Jeffrey is also an author of several books, the first of which, The Psychic in You published one of my spirit photographs for the hardcover release.

Interestingly, the Portrait uncovered within that photo became one of the favorites I mentioned earlier. It's also interesting that even after twenty years no one's ever seen it. I'm not surprised, it's actually hidden quite well, you wouldn't realize it was even there.

Jeffrey played a big part in my decision to shoot spirit photography as he constantly suggested I visit the cemetery with my camera. He later gave me the old, "I told you so" speech when I returned with positive results. We had many late night discussions after I sent him emails with attachments of my new captures.

Mostly, I took care of Jeffrey's website; I was into tech and worked as a freelance programmer. It was mutual, I needed an interesting subject to practice my creative developments skills and Jeffrey needed creative development skills. Problem solved.

My corporate background was in application development for mainframe computers using BAL 370, but my favorite platform was working with multimedia; digital audio, video, animation graphics, and the Internet. Multimedia development software were my favorite apps.

Back in the 90's website development was hands-on, very different than it is now with automatic templates and drag n drop interfaces. The Internet was also in its infancy and far from the current standards and objectives, especially in server technology. And it was expensive; I made good money back then, but not off my friends, they just paid expenses. Luckily I had very few friends.

I believe the first website we put online for Jeff was higherminds-radio.com. As I said, he was hosting a psychic call-in show. There was a point, early in the 2000's, when he was Live on WLIR FM radio, Live on the Internet and Live in the chat room all from a computer I stoked into his website from my basement. I'd gotten a static IP address from my Internet provider and was running a web server from a second machine at my house. I pre-programmed the pages on Jeffrey's site to accept my server address and set up a chat room. Then to pump the live radio broadcast through the homepage on the website, I took a live feed from the radio and input that into my local server. When Jeff went live, I swapped out the buttons on the homepage and… live audio stream.

There was also a Tarot page where you could get a reading from the computer. It was a three or five card spread, your choice. I used random numbers to generate cards and display interpretations. Back then I was very familiar with Tarot. I scanned a popular deck for the card images and programmed the logic in a common scripting language.

Later on, we incorporated download pages. Jeffrey had many celebrity clients and friends, sometimes they'd come to the station for live interviews. Jeff would get tapes of all his shows, we did a little editing and put the highlights online for download upon request. We did the same for some of his television spots, though video was a much bigger issue then than it is now. We even had a page highlighting my photography …it was a great website.

Eventually, I gave up freelance programming and went back to corporate life and a steady paycheck as a multimedia developer working in mid-town Manhattan. Jeffrey made other arrangements and continues to maintain a comprehensive Internet, radio and in-person presence at book signings and events.

Looking back after twenty five years and remembering the technology struggles and triumphs, I can honestly say we did not squander any opportunities to bring it. Jeffrey's web presence had the bells and whistles to get you interested and content to keep you coming back for more, and it still does.

A Shared Space

End of life, and the afterlife, nothing is more intriguing, nothing is more baffling. Death affects every human being that has walked or will walk on this earth, and yet we continue to rely on superstition, legends, myths and folklore for answers to the most common questions: What happens when we die? Is there an afterlife? If there is a spirit world why can't we see them? Where is the proof of the hereafter?

For many of us these questions are answered through religious teachings and beliefs. All major religions speak of a spiritual hereafter that awaits us when we die. A promise of an existence beyond what we know. These beliefs have been passed along in hundreds of cultures for thousands of years. Since written records have been kept, men have written about the eternal hereafter, the invisible world inhabited by our long lines of deceased ancestors, the dwelling place of angelic beings, demonic spirits, and ghosts.

The spirit world, an ancient and mysterious dwelling place revered by some and feared by others. All believing their traditional system of knowledge was the extent of the hereafter. The cultural and geographical differences have provided some interesting legends over the past several thousand years of recorded history.

The ancient Egyptians paved their way to the afterlife by burying themselves with as much treasure as was befitting their individual social status and even contrived spells to help with the passage to the afterlife. In the case of the lesser fortunate members of their society, their reward in the afterlife was based on their service to the social elite.

The Native American Indians of North and South America believed the spirit world was a part of everyday life and communicated with their deceased ancestors daily. They believed the spirit world naturally interacted with the real world as a normal daily occurrence. They also recognized certain individuals in their tribes or clans to possess spiritual abilities more advanced than most others, eventually they would evolve as the spiritual leaders.

The Roman Catholics believe a spiritual afterlife is a promise made to mankind by Jesus Christ. They believe that mankind will someday be awakened from death to encounter Judgment Day, and the followers of Jesus will be raised to Heaven and all others are to be banished to Hell along with the devil where they shall encounter eternal suffering.

These are just a few of the many cultural belief systems that have perpetrated man's imagination pertaining to the afterlife. Why is it imagination? Because none of these belief systems have ever provided tangible proof that their system is The System.

It's not that we don't think about it almost every day. Some of the greatest minds in history have contemplated death and the hereafter and have given us nothing more than philosophical conjecture, superstitious dogma or opinions that can best be described as wishful thinking.

Some of the greatest religious figures in history have made promises of transition to a wonderful existence in the next world, but this is really nothing more than words and cushions for people who seek comfort when facing the sad inevitable face of death.

An afterlife existence at best is a presumptuous opinion based on faith. Religious inspiration may provide comfort to many as is evident from the endless streams of people rallying to churches, synagogues, and mosques throughout the world, but then there are also those who require a more logical if not factual reason to consider the possibility another more reasonable and peaceful existence awaits us when we die.

How wonderful it would be if we could prepare our immortal soul for the transition to the next world much as we do when planning for old age and retirement. Imagine yourself contributing to the salvation of your soul much as you would your 401k or social security benefits.

The Bible declares you can do just that, unfortunately, no one has been able to substantiate such claims. To begin with no one has been able to provide evidence of an immortal soul. Of course if the existence of a soul were to be provided it would in turn necessitate a form of afterlife existence. The evidence of one would substantiate the existence of the other.

Many of us have wondered if there was an afterlife "what would it be like?" If we could move past the sticking point of proof, if we could realize there is an existence of spiritual beings sharing space with us, or us with them, then comes the truly exciting part of the journey, examination of the inhabitants in their own environment. This I believe would be the next great form of human endeavors, exploration of the invisible world of spirits.

Consider for a moment the crossing of the great oceans in a time when superstition and fear ruled the majority of society. It was thought certain death at the hands of evil spirits and mythical monsters awaited those who ventured into the vastness of the seas and oceans. But some men did it, they ventured out into the unknown. That same unknown we now cross hundreds if not thousands of times daily not only by sea but by air as well.

To some it may seem ridiculous such primitive thoughts and superstitious beliefs ruled the hearts and minds of men. But are modern philosophies any different now when it comes to the existence of the spirit world? It doesn't necessarily mean some of us must literally return from the dead to revisit this domain. But it does mean in order to gain a greater understanding of the natural or supernatural world we must overcome the fear and superstitions that still prevail when it comes to the hereafter.

If we are to someday avail ourselves of positive interactions with a form of nature that may exist, then someone needs to step up to the plate and remove the fear and superstition from the equation and level the playing field.

Baseball has a saying, "take one for the team." You step up to the plate and get hit with a fastball thrown at 90+ MPH, yeah it's going to hurt, but we need to get on base and score a run. In baseball, when a pitch is thrown close to the batter they jump out of the way because it really hurts to get nailed with a fastball. But in order to move forward with your larger objective it might cause you a little pain and suffering along the way, ergo …take one for the team.

I use the term "exploration" because to me the spirit world is uncharted territory. Many of us believe something is there. Thousands of cultures over thousands of years believed it too. And when it comes to the spirit world the entrenched religions often win over the masses with promises of Heaven or threats of Hell. Many lives firmly entrenched around the world will resist contrary or obstructive ideas. Well not here, and not now.

Because, this is where legitimate, logical and compulsive evidence will take root. As entrenched in superstitious or religious belief as many of us are (myself included), facts are difficult to ignore amongst reasonable people. When dealing with spirits, any evidence may be attributed to being the work of evil spirits and rejected upon that basis, once again, not here, and not now.

Such has been the case in the past when psychics and spirit mediums have performed incredible acts of unexplainable communications. Why? Because it's what we've been taught for over two thousand years, that contact with spirits is the work of devilish or demonic forces.

At least it's an acknowledgment the spirits exist. We can deal with the philosophical concept of good and evil the same way the explorers of the unknown oceans handled the evil monsters of their day, with guts, determination to succeed and a logical mind that will not abide by superstition and fear.

It can be a cold and lonely road when traveling in condemnation by the religious majority. No one, and I mean no one, I know wants to be considered as being in league with evil or demonic forces. We should know for ourselves what our true intentions are and proceed according to our own hearts and minds.

Many rely on the Bible for comfort when facing the inevitability of death. But of course in a logical and technologically advanced society such as ours, is it outrageous to say the Bible cannot be considered as factual no matter how many people claim the Bible is the foregone word of God? It must be taken on faith. There's that word again, "faith." Well, faith may move mountains but it certainly does not provide evidence or proof of what may or may not await us in the hereafter.

So is the Bible a source worth considering? Absolutely. In addition to its teachings of peace, love and hope, it contains an abundance of spiritual information. And even though much of its contents cannot be confirmed scientifically, historically it provides a basis, a foundation and a starting point from which you can begin to negotiate the truth from the legends and the myths.

Whether you choose to consider it as gospel truth or literary fantasy, it does in fact purport to reveal esoteric knowledge in great detail of the spirit world. According to the Bible, not only is there an afterlife but it differentiates the inhabitants to suffer appropriate levels and outcomes according to the quality of the soul.

It speaks of the reward of heavenly bliss for those that have lived a just and God fearing life, and promising an existence of torment and punishment for those who have performed corruptible deeds.

Apparently, there is an authority that will be determining a reward or punishment for incoming souls. It appears there is a hierarchy of super spiritual beings controlling the spiritual realm. So it not only advances the existence of an afterlife, it's giving us an inside view of spirit politics.

Another interesting concept is although the Bible may be one of the most proficient sources of information on spirits and the spirit world, it strictly forbids communication with the inhabitants residing in that spirit world. Of course some people take the Bible literally and go no further when it pertains to spirit communication… some people.

There are many who may believe uncovering knowledge of the spirit world is a gift that should be looked upon favorably. The possibility that a fresh set of ideas used in attaining spiritual knowledge is not only a gift to be shared, it's a responsibility to be explored. I find these terms acceptable.

Historically, we have displayed little or no ability when it comes to identifying a spirit as being good or evil. It is said, a spirit who wishes to perform an evil act is capable of disguising his true intentions. I see that as a problem for us. I have spoken to many people who feel they are fully capable of differentiating between good and evil spirits.

I think some people think too much of their abilities in comparison to the psychological effectiveness that a spiritual intelligence possibly older and more cunning than can be comprehended by any man …or woman. This type of overconfidence should be examined carefully if we are to remain grounded and logical in our attempt to gain understanding of a spiritual afterlife, or an anomalous consciousness of super-nature.

The Biblical reference to the occupation of the earth by an army of fallen angels may not only be possible but probable. This army is said to be controlled by the super spirit known as "Satan." He is the enemy of mankind and uses his army of fallen angels to exert his will.

For those seeking experiences with the spirit world, it helps to know who you might meet along the way. Having accurate renditions of those legends and myths allows for mental preparation of the unknown. Consider it a starting point for spiritual exploration.

There are many sources of information available to help provoke an imaginative sense of spiritual awakening. There's no formula, some might consider additional forms of religious material, others may consider material of a more mystical or occult nature. The point is to awaken in you the will to find your own spiritual path.

The Bible is not the only reference for spirit activity. There have been many interesting and intriguing concepts revealed in the works of authors such as Dante's Inferno, where he describes a visionary passage through Hell while accompanied by his guide and good buddy, Virgil.

In his travels through the levels and inner circles of Hell he speaks of seeing the tormented souls of sinners as they spend eternity in torturous regret of past misdeeds. He finally happens upon the maligned spirit of the Devil called Lucifer and describes him as being a three headed beast frozen up to his waist and surrounded by a cloudy mist. Hmmm

Dante's visionary work is written to be a poem. Considering the time in which it was written, anything other than a work of fiction might have caused him to have his head cut off, burned alive, or both. That US Constitution is lookin' pretty good about now isn't it?

Another defining and informative work was written in 1975 by Dr. Raymond Moody. He revealed a groundbreaking study of the Near Death Experience. In his book "Life after Life", Dr. Moody performed interviews with dozens of persons purported to have been clinically dead for up to several minutes, only to be revived, and then, described what they thought was entry into the afterlife.

Most if not all of these persons were consistent and shared their descriptions of passing through a tunnel and emerging into the presence of a bright light. They were greeted by deceased relatives or friends and in some cases thought they were in the presence of an almighty being.

These persons having recovered from their brush with death were said to have vivid recollections of the hereafter and their lives were changed forever. For them the existence of an afterlife is not only real it is inevitable.

Still others choose to seek out psychics or spirit mediums to satisfy their search for answers. Psychics and mediums have at times displayed immense abilities of spirit communication. Psychic visions of heaven and hell, near death experiences or divine intervention through angelic forces have become a huge part of the spiritual arena.

It would certainly appear some are indeed communicating with an intelligent being in possession of private or restricted information only they can deliver. To the recipient of the information and to the observers as well, it appears the psychic is communicating with a ghost or spirit.

Some have become convincingly accurate in obtaining quality information. The competition is aggressive and the need for accuracy is mandatory. In some cases even the most skeptical viewer would leave the session or demonstration scratching their head and wondering if what they just witnessed was legitimately supernatural or just a complex and elaborate hoax.

Still, those who require more tangible evidence before committing themselves to believing in a spiritual afterlife, psychic mediumship will not suffice. No matter how convincing, compelling or accurate a story or performance may be, without some type of tangible evidence of the communicative event, it remains just that, a story or a performance. Could it be the evidence being sought has not been found because it's been hiding in the safest place:

...in plain sight.

...a thousand words

The Devil's in the Details

Sometimes I just go to say "hello", no camera, no recorder and no hunting. I imagine it gets lonely if no one ever visits them, so I pay my respects to the dead ones; it makes me feel good to do it. I also like the peaceful atmosphere and solitude, there's no place quite like them.

I live near an infamous cemetery in CT. It's on church grounds, and at night, it's patrolled by the local police. The first time I went there they got me, and since I'm too old to get arrested for trespassing I decided the best move would be to take the high road, I said, thanks for the heads up, have good night.

I have gone back there in the daytime, in an attempt to experience EVP (electronic voice phenomena). My method for an EVP session is simple, no talking. Mind your own business, keep your mouth shut, and keep walkin'. I got several responses for my efforts. Those are the only times I've tried to capture EVP, it was interesting to witness it happen, and I can attest to its authenticity. It can be an interesting experience.

I captured one female voice who called me by name; she said it was "nice to meet ya", that was cool. I have another female who just said "help me", almost desperately. That was sad. Others had stronger voices in db, but unintelligible words. I will admit to using some of my EVPs in a few studio versions of songs I've written. It was too cool to pass up. I had to do it. I'm glad I did, it sounds great.

I don't do cemeteries anymore unless I have a good reason, or asked by a friend. I think some spirits are there for whatever reason God only knows. But I don't believe they are tied to their decaying bodies unless they are forced by some unknown means to do so. And if they are, it's not my business.

Spirits travel; I believe they have no bounds that we recognize unless they apply them to themselves, or have them applied by other more powerful forces. Lesser developed souls might feel the need to hang around their own rotting corpses, whether they like it or not. And again, it's not my business.

Maybe a hundred years from now some character will visit my grave for no other reason than to say "Hey Jim, how are the worms treating you?" If indeed I was there, I would grab them around the ankles and tell them, "come back with some cigarettes and whiskey, we can hang." I've tried to keep an open mind and an honest attitude during my reflections. Knowing is learning, learning is a lifelong process. Some say multiple lifetimes. Sadly, not all of it is by choice …others may disagree.

Interpretations such as this one are to be expected. Detail is a subjective opinion; in a case such as this, trying to establish an empirical explanation for the occurrences may prove difficult, many anomalous experiences often remain unexplained.

I'm aware it may have been stubbornness, pride or both compelling me to continue my efforts and I was grateful. I knew they were close, and soon they would begin to appear. I remain convinced the option to appear is not of our choosing. However, I do feel a human factor is a necessary element. So I waited…

You should be standing very still when you face them. The slightest movement causes them to vanish. I stood motionless for as long as possible, not blinking until my eyes burned with pain. I even tried to slow the blood flowing through my veins so the noise wouldn't give me away …and I waited.

I thought if they believed I was sleeping they'd come closer, trying to get a good look. I wouldn't call it a trick; it's more of an alert system methodology, part of my safety program initiative.

At times, adversarial thoughts are natural occurrences and boundaries become tested, by both parties. So you stand by motionless, with your finger on the trigger, ready to shoot trespassers, transgressors, and ghosts if they come 'cross the line.

Sometimes there are recognizable anatomical features, structures, and colors, and strange misty fogs with defined shapes, all appearing and disappearing instantly.

The anomalous material appears to be a vaporous exotic energy that supports a conscious existence in ways we've never imagined. I've begun to notice the color shadings and values often consist of reds, whites and …blues. I take that as a positive sign.

I'm comfortable with the "I've seen a few" point of view. As far as what is reflected in the photograph, I can only consider it to be a pure ghost or a spirit, or, what I understand a ghost or spirit might be. Entire lifetimes are wasted not getting past this particular sticking point.

My resolve to pursue this avenue of discovery would be tested often, eventually becoming a timeless effort of sacrifice and determination to overcome many obstacles. It's been said, dramatic efforts are expected in order to obtain dramatic results. I agree.

When I realized them to be the rare and unique entities they are, I began experimenting on them like a mad scientist on a mission …often wondering what DaVinci, Nostradamus, or Jesus would have accomplished with a state of the art personal computer system, the Internet …and a score to settle.

I originally developed the term "Spiritography" as the name for my personal catalog of spirit photography and images. Spiritography uses state of the art computers instead of shovels and a toothbrush to reveal the hidden treasure, the ultimate treasure, the Book of Portraits.

Well …it's been great talking with you. These photographs as well as any photographs may be interpreted any number of ways. A spirit definition is a personal one, I feel lucky to have seen them, and shot them. Sorry, but I have to go now, the suns coming up…

The traps are full again.

C'mere, let me show you…

The End

"C'mere, let me show you…"

Portraits 5.1

Afterword

Afterword

My efforts in spirit photography were conducted in an attempt to witness and record authentic supernatural occurrences. At times, the experiments were successful. I'm convinced the photographs contain compelling evidence of an afterlife or alternate existence.

Some anomalies appear with features similar to humans, but they're not. I make no attempt to render an explanation or interpretation on the origin of the anomalies. That is better left to the experts.

Success or failure in spirit photography can spin on a dime. If you're resourceful enough to obtain a controlled and secure environment you may increase your chances of success. Even still, the rarity of a spirit manifestation will seriously try your patience.

I believe it was a mutual experience. I imagine having to pass several tests before I was invited to participate in the secret club. After that, we had fun with it, many showed up to participate in the activities …and have their picture taken.

My philosophy is simple, if there's information out there, and the only way to find it - is to go out there and look for it, then if I'm the one going out there I'm bringing traps.

…it sends a message to the other ghosts

When it started to work I wanted more. So I went for it… I set more traps and it fkn worked. I nailed them again and again, after a while I got tired of it, and I left them alone. I wasn't the only one, they were doing it too. They sneak right up on you, and get you when you're not looking. I had to get them back. In my mind, it became a game.

Like most people I tend to draw inspiration from historical figures and situations. However, in order to advance the accepted concepts of spirit research, technology has placed computers and various forms of digital equipment in our hands.

In actuality computers simply execute the thoughts and will from the mind of the programmer. Over the years, I've experimented with this concept to help me capture and identify ghosts and spirits, and to develop more than a few software systems when I was at work.

I believe I offer an accurate interpretation of this phenomenon. The PC's advancements over these decades have been like ordering a magical machine from God's private catalog. That's when I considered subliminal influences and interpretations …and what it could do to you if someone evil thought of it first.

~ Jim ~

*"It's like trying to catch a bird in your hands with your eyes closed.
It can be done if you wait long enough
…until they're comfortable."*

Portraits 6.1

Appendices

…a thousand words

APPENDICES

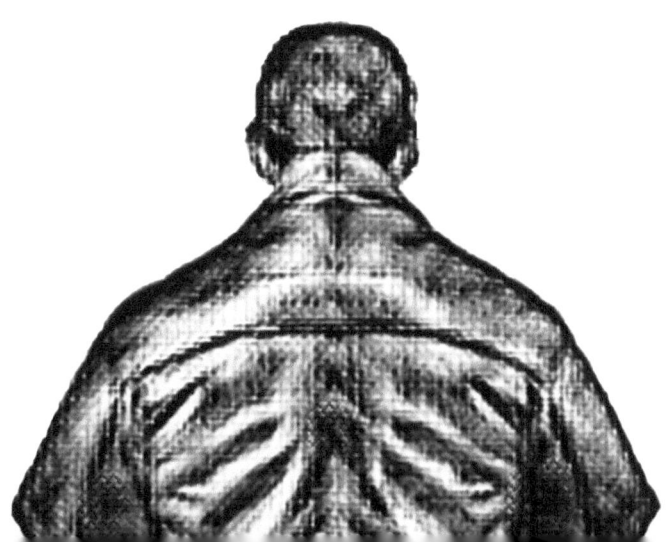

Appendix A:

List of Photographs

1.	PA015011	page 12
2.	PB017303	page 16
3.	PB017306	page 17
4.	PB017322	page 18
5.	PA065312	page 20
6.	P9111813	page 22
7.	PA201971	page 24
8.	PC171678	page 25
9.	P1011589	page 26
10.	PB231607	page 27
11.	P8100098	page 28
12.	Pb017297	page 29
13.	P1010255	page 30
14.	PA202007	page 31
15.	PA201995	page 32
16.	P1010091	page 33
17.	PA201956	page 34
18.	P1018258	page 35
19.	P1010119	page 36
20.	PA126211	page 37
21.	PA065358	page 38
22.	P1019319	page 39
23.	PA201746	page 40
24.	PA201723	page 41
25.	P1010069	page 42
26.	PA065373	page 43
27.	PA065283	page 44
28.	P1019319	page 55

...a thousand words

List of Portraits

1.	Wings of the Wind	page 57
2.	T-Bone / Wyatt	page 58
3.	Fingers / King Dragon	page 59
4.	James / Chief	page 60
5.	Lord of the Seven Days / Beast of the Angels	page 61
6.	Djra-Kul-A-Din / Spirit of the Second Sight	page 62
7.	Hammerhead / Flag	page 63
8.	Fang / ChilliPop	page 64
9.	Instant Karma / Dr. Seven	page 65
10.	Karats / Endora	page 66
11.	The Drip / Sparx	page 67
12.	Aquadio / Prince Dragon	page 68
13.	John the Elder / Ace	page 69
14.	Bones	page 70
15.	T-Bone	page 71
16.	Wyatt	page 74
17.	Fingers	page 77
18.	King Dragon	page 80
19.	James	page 83
20.	Djra-Kul-A-Din	page 85
21.	Chief	page 86
22.	Endora	page 88
23.	Fang	page 89
24.	Beast of the Angels	page 90
25.	Instant Karma	page 91
26.	Lord of the Seven Days	page 92
27.	Sparx	page 94
28.	Wings of the Wind	page 95
29.	John the Elder	page 97
30.	Hammerhead	page 98
31.	Flag	page 99
32.	ChilliPop	page 100
33.	The Drip	page 101
34.	Aquadio	page 102
35.	Spirit of the Second Sight	page 103
36.	Dr. Seven	page 104
37.	Ace	page 105
38.	Karats	page 106
39.	Prince Dragon	page 107
40.	Bones	page 108

List of Illustrations

1.	JD / Wyatt	page 1
2.	JD / Chief	page 9
3.	JD / LSD	page 49
4.	JD / Fingers	page 113
5.	JD / Wings	page 143

Appendix B:

Spiritography

"Spiritography," is my collection of spirit photographs and images. Period. Full Stop. End of Story.

The name came to me while I was waking up one morning. That is a fact. After searching the Internet and finding zero results… I searched the U.S. Library of Congress and the U.S. Copyright Office again finding zero results. I registered the domain name:

Spiritography.com

Spiritography.com
Creation Date: 2001-03-12
08:53:34

I registered with the U.S. Copyright Office.

Type of Work: Visual Material
Registration Number / Date: VAu000563462 / 2002-08-23
Title: Spiritography : vol. 1.
Description: Photos.
Copyright Claimant: James DeCaro
Date of Creation: 2001

I'd say that makes it mine. Period. Full Stop. End of Story. It's really the only way to preserve authenticity. Facts are facts, all of them count.

...a thousand words

Appendix C:

Cameras / Computers / Digital Equipment

I use a digital camera because that's what I have. I used two brand new digital cameras usually set to AS400 film speed. No special lens or shutter speeds, just stock equipment. It doesn't take a nuclear fueled heat seeking infrared lens to take a picture of a ghost. It takes a ghost.

2.1 Megapixel Digital Cameras
Computers - Digital Tablet & Pen

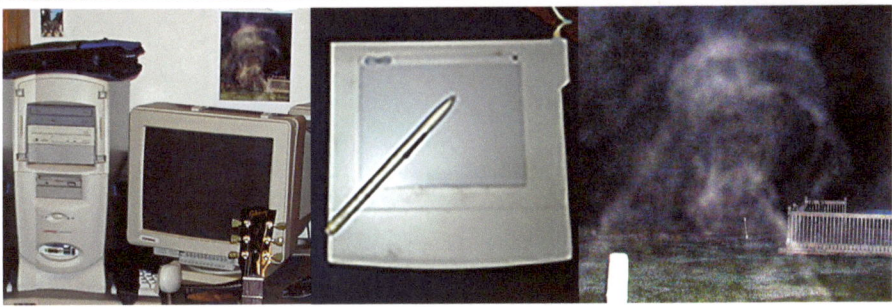

(T) Cameras   (L) Computer   (C) Tablet   (R) The Ghost

Appendix D:

Bibliography / References

Anderson, G. (1988) We Don't Die, George Anderson's Conversations with the Other Side, Putnam

Belanger, J. (2005) Communicating with the Dead: Reach Beyond the Grave, Red Wheel/Weiser, Career Press, Incorporated (p75-77)

CBS News Productions, (2005) Mediums: we see dead people, A&E Network

DeCaro, J - Walker, D. (1982) The End, Soundscape Long Island, Kewall

FATE (Jan. 2008) Celebrating 60 years, FATE Magazine, Inc.

Moody, R. (1975) Life After Life: the investigation of a phenomenon – survival of bodily death, San Francisco, CA: HarperSanFrancisco, 2001

Storm, L. (2001) Photographic anomalies on the internet, International Journal of Parapsychology 50th anniversary Edition, Parapsychology Foundation, Inc. (p197-198)

Wands, J. (2004) The Psychic In You (Hardcover), Atria (p227-234)

Appendix E:

Sunrise

...end of life, the soul separates from the body likely retaining traces of a human scent. The remaining human scent is burned away on the coming sunrise. How much it's going to burn is between you and God. If the human scent is not incinerated the soul remains earth bound. After the second sunrise they become half-breeds ...ghosts, wandering the earth for eternity. Based upon their half-breed existence ghosts are shunned by both humans and spirits. They exist in darkness and instinctively evade the new sunrise. As long as the human scent lingers over their souls, they are destined to wander the earth. Realizing their place in the universe may cause them to become angry, despondent, neglected and hopelessly lost. They may inadvertently or intentionally begin to haunt the earth. When they do the hunters are released. The hunters follow the scent of human remains ...like animals.

...a thousand words

...a thousand words

Spiritography and the Book of Portraits

Jim DeCaro

...thanks for reading.

...*a thousand words*

~ JD ~

"The hunters follow the scent of human remains …like animals."

Portraits 7.1

Index

Index

A

alternate dimensions 9, 10
anomalistic psychology xvii
anomalous phenomena 2, 4, 106
apparition 1, 9

B

Beatles 117
Beringian 33
Bible 53
Book of Portraits 29, 49, 50, 51, 53, 70, 138

C

Camera
  cameras xvii, 106, 153
capnomancy xviii
Catholicism 115
Cherubim 95
complex spirit interpretation 49

D

Daniel, Book of 53
Dante's Inferno 133
dark dimensions 103
discarnate entity 9
DNA
  DNA 14, 32, 33, 40, 50, 84
  DNA factors 38, 83
Donny Walker 117

E

Ectoplasm
  ectoplasm 11, 14, 35, 39, 83
  Ectoplasm: theory of emanations 11, 14, 35
EVP 135
Ezekiel, Book of 53

F

Fallen Angel 90

G

George Anderson 120
George Patton xix
Ghost 20
  Ghosthunter 20, 21
  Ghost Hunting 20
  ghosts 1, 2, 3, 9, 13, 21, 22

H

higher dimensions 103
human element 37
Hun-Tdey 12

I

illusionary capabilities 83
illusions 1

J

James Walker and the Creeps 117
JD 57
Jeffrey Wands 123
John 119

K

Ka-bar 29
King Dragon 80

L

Life after Life 133
liquid smoke 107

M

materialize
  materialization 23, 52

materialization process 107
materialized spirit matter 107
mechanism of natural deception 55
Mesopotamia 41
multi-force phenomenon 97
multiverse theory 9

N

Native American xviii, 33, 40, 41, 128

O

objective field 37, 38

P

Parallel rules 50
pareidolia xvii
Psychomanteum 121

R

Raymond Moody xvii, 121
Revelation, Book of 53

S

scenting 99
spinner 108
Spiritography 1, 4, 152
Spiritography.com 152
spirit photography xvii, 31, 122, 123, 138, 143
sub-dimensions 10
supernatural illusions 2, 55, 71
super-nature 55, 114, 132

T

telepathic 103, 123
Theater of the Mind Research Center 121
The Creeps 117
the line 10
traps 20, 21, 138, 144

U

USA 114
US Constitution 115
U.S. Copyright Office 152
U.S. Library of Congress 152

W

Warrior culture 29
Wings 53, 57, 89, 92, 93, 95, 96
wizard 17, 18

www.spiritography.com

www.ingramcontent.com/pod-product-compliance
Lightning Source LLC
Chambersburg PA
CBHW041457010526
44119CB00023B/383/J